It's another Quality Book from CGP

This book is for anyone doing GCSE Modern World History.

Whatever subject you're doing it's the same
old story — there are lots of facts and you've just got
to learn them. KS4 History is no different.

Happily this CGP book gives you all that important
information as clearly and concisely as possible.

It's also got some daft bits in to try and make the whole
experience at least vaguely entertaining for you.

What CGP is all about

Our sole aim here at CGP is to produce the highest quality books
— carefully written, immaculately presented and dangerously
close to being funny.

Then we work our socks off to get them out to you
— at the cheapest possible prices.

Contents

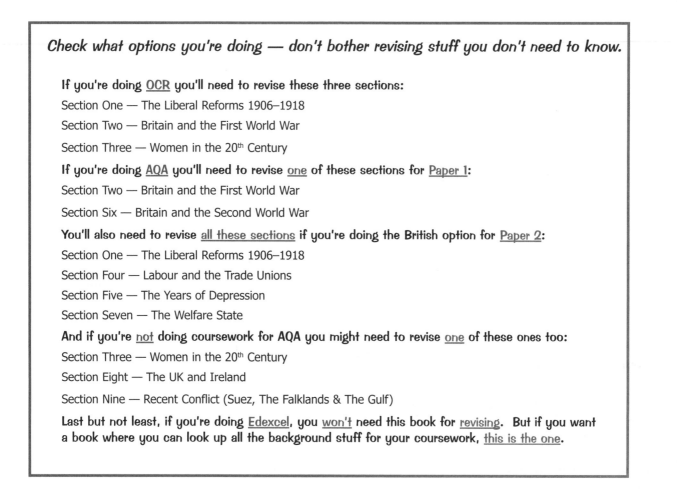

Check what options you're doing — don't bother revising stuff you don't need to know.

If you're doing <u>OCR</u> you'll need to revise these three sections:

Section One — The Liberal Reforms 1906–1918

Section Two — Britain and the First World War

Section Three — Women in the 20ᵗʰ Century

If you're doing <u>AQA</u> you'll need to revise <u>one</u> of these sections for <u>Paper 1</u>:

Section Two — Britain and the First World War

Section Six — Britain and the Second World War

You'll also need to revise <u>all these sections</u> if you're doing the British option for <u>Paper 2</u>:

Section One — The Liberal Reforms 1906–1918

Section Four — Labour and the Trade Unions

Section Five — The Years of Depression

Section Seven — The Welfare State

And if you're <u>not</u> doing coursework for AQA you might need to revise <u>one</u> of these ones too:

Section Three — Women in the 20ᵗʰ Century

Section Eight — The UK and Ireland

Section Nine — Recent Conflict (Suez, The Falklands & The Gulf)

Last but not least, if you're doing <u>Edexcel</u>, you <u>won't</u> need this book for <u>revising</u>. But if you want a book where you can look up all the background stuff for your coursework, <u>this is the one</u>.

Published by Coordination Group Publications Ltd.

Contributors:

David Barnes

Simon Cook

Taissa Csáky

Gemma Hallam

Alison Palin

Kat Stewart

ISBN: 978 1 84146 302 5

Groovy website: www.cgpbooks.co.uk
Jolly bits of clipart from CorelDRAW®
Printed by Elanders Hindson Ltd, Newcastle upon Tyne.

The Need for Reform

In 1900 many people in Britain weren't just a bit poor, they were desperate. There was no Government help for the old, ill or unemployed. At the same time, a great debate was going on about whether the Government had a duty to help these people, or a duty not to interfere in their lives.

Poor people *faced serious hardship in 1900*

1) The only help available for very poor people was workhouses run by local councils. In the workhouses people worked long hours in brutal conditions for basic food and lodging. Many people saw going to the workhouse as the end of all self-respect and preferred to starve.

2) There was serious unemployment in some industries, and no 'dole' or unemployment benefit. If you were out of work you had to get by on nothing at all, or go into the workhouse.

3) Old people who had no savings or family to help them suffered very badly — there were no government pensions. The only option for many old people was the workhouse.

4) Housing in poor areas was damp, cold and didn't have proper sewage systems. It was easy to get ill in these conditions, and illness meant missing work, and maybe losing your job.

5) Many people couldn't afford doctors or medicine.

6) Many children had to go out to work from an early age, and so missed out on getting an education.

7) Large numbers of people couldn't even afford to eat properly. Out of all the men recruited to fight in the Boer War (1899-1902), half were malnourished.

Two reports said a third of British people were poor

Not everybody believed that poverty was all that bad — especially not rich people. Two reports said that poverty was serious, and that it affected large numbers of people.

1) Seebohm Rowntree had a factory in York. He didn't believe there were serious problems, so he did a survey of living conditions. He found that 28% of people in York were so poor that they couldn't afford basic food and housing. The report of the survey, called "*Poverty, a study of town life*" was published in 1901.

Talk about how the other two thirds lives...

2) Charles Booth published "*Life and Labour of the People in London*" in 1903. This showed that 30% of people in London were living in severe poverty. Booth's report also showed that it was sometimes impossible for people to find work, however hard they tried. He also showed that wages for some jobs were so low that they weren't enough to support a family.

Public opinion *on helping poor people* began to change

There was no way you could put a third of the population into the workhouse. Britain needed a new approach to dealing with poverty. Plenty of people had an opinion on how it should be done.

1) Popular and well-respected writers like George Bernard Shaw, J.Galsworthy and H.G.Wells described how poor people lived in their books. They said the poor members of society needed help, and the Government should pass laws to make sure it happened.

2) People involved in public health and medicine said the Government should get more involved in health issues.

3) Socialists argued that wealth should be more equally spread between working people, and people like factory owners and land owners, who were traditionally the richest.

4) The Labour Party was the only main political party that was enthusiastic about socialist ideas. They argued that the Government should give financial help to the poorest members of society. Labour was attracting more and more working-class supporters.

Rowntree — social reformer AND inventor of Fruit Gums...

What a cracker of a page. Learn the examples of the problems facing poor people, the two reports, and the new ideas on helping the poor. Scribble them down, and check you've got them right.

Conservatives, Liberals and Labour

Pressure was growing for the Government to deal with poverty. The main parties — the Liberals and the Conservatives — traditionally felt that it wasn't the Government's role. But things were changing.

The political parties had very different attitudes to poverty

The oldest, most powerful political parties — the Liberals and the Conservatives — didn't really agree with giving government help to people. They believed that:

1) the Government should interfere as little as possible in people's lives;
2) people should be free to decide how to spend their money, so it was wrong to raise taxes;
3) giving poor people money was morally wrong as it undermined their independence.

The Labour Party didn't have many MPs before 1906, but they did have growing support from working people. They believed that:

1) the poorest people in society should get Government help;
2) the Government should get the cash to pay for this from taxes;
3) the Government should also take over (nationalise) the major industries and make use of the profits.

Some Liberals, and some Conservatives were more open to the idea of the Government helping the poor — especially if it helped their party win votes from Labour.

A Royal Commission investigated poverty

In 1905 the Conservative government set up a Royal Commission to look at the Poor Law. This was a nineteenth century law which had set up the workhouses and other help for the poor. The Commission was supposed to decide whether the help given by the Poor Law was good enough. But the members of the Commission couldn't agree about what caused poverty so they published two reports:

The Majority Report (what the majority of the commission thought)
- *If people were poor it was their own fault.*
- *They made themselves poor by gambling and drinking, so they didn't deserve help.*
- *Enough was being done for the poor already.*

The Minority Report (what the minority of the commission thought)
- *People couldn't help being poor.*
- *Illness, old age, and a shortage of jobs made people poor.*
- *They thought more should be done to prevent people being poor.*

After 1906 the Liberals brought in social reforms

1) In 1906 the Liberal Party won a landslide general election victory over the Conservatives.

2) At the same election 29 Labour Party MPs were elected to the House of Commons. They were now in a good position to push for help for the poor.

3) The Minority Report, combined with pressure from the general public, and the pressure from the Labour Party encouraged the Liberals to bring laws in that would deal with poverty.

4) The Liberals also wanted to compete with the Labour Party. They were worried about losing support from working-class voters. They felt new policies would appeal directly to the people.

5) The poor physical condition of working-class volunteers for the Boer War had shocked many. If Britain were involved in a major war, it would need a healthy working class to fight as soldiers.

6) David Lloyd George and Winston Churchill* were the MPs who worked hardest to drive the bills through. They wanted to help the poor, but they were also keen to make a name for themselves.

The Liberal reforms — what were the real reasons...

We're used to the idea of benefits and pensions being paid by the Government but at the time this was a new idea. Scribble down the reasons why the Liberals brought in social reforms after 1906.

* Watch out for Churchill — he was a Liberal until the 1920s when he became a Conservative.

Laws to Help Children and Old People

The Liberals <u>didn't plan</u> to help <u>everyone</u> — just the people with the <u>worst problems</u>. They were: children from poor families, old people, ill people, and people who were out of work or badly paid. Unfortunately they've left you <u>reams of laws</u> to learn...

Children needed special protection

In <u>1906</u> the <u>School Meals Act</u> allowed <u>LEAs</u> to supply <u>free</u> school meals paid for out of <u>rates</u>.

<u>LEAs</u> = Local Education Authorities. They were in charge of running state schools.

<u>rates</u> = local council tax

In <u>1907</u> LEAs started giving children at their schools <u>free medical inspections</u>. Many of them built clinics where they could hold the inspections.

I think it was the sprouts.

In <u>1908</u> Parliament passed the <u>Children's Charter</u> to give children some legal protection. The Charter made it illegal for children younger than <u>16</u> to <u>buy cigarettes</u>, <u>go into a pub</u> or <u>beg</u>.

<u>Herbert Samuel</u> from the Home Office tried to help <u>young offenders</u>:

1) He set up <u>Borstals</u> — special prisons for young offenders so they wouldn't have to go to adult prisons.

2) He set up the <u>probation service</u> to try to keep young people from reoffending.

Old people got state pensions

In <u>1908</u> <u>David Lloyd George</u> was Chancellor of the Exchequer. He introduced the <u>Old Age Pensions Act</u>. These are the most important bits of the Act.

1) The pension was for people <u>over 70</u> on low incomes.

2) The scheme was <u>non-contributory</u> — you didn't have to pay money in to get a pension when you retired. The pensions were paid for by money raised through <u>ordinary taxes</u>.

3) In the <u>1908</u> budget <u>£1 200 000</u> of tax money was set aside to pay for pensions.

4) Single people with an income of <u>less than £21 per year</u> got 5 shillings per week. <u>Married couples</u> with an income of <u>less than £21 per year</u> got 7s 6d (7 shillings & 6 pence) per week.

5) Anyone whose income was <u>between £21 and £31 per year</u> got a smaller pension.

6) People with an income of <u>over £31</u> per year didn't get a pension at all.

7) The first pensions ever were paid on <u>1ˢᵗ January 1909</u>.

Although Labour said 5 shillings was <u>too little</u>, the pension was <u>immensely popular</u>. Lloyd George took the <u>credit</u>.

Remember the aim <u>wasn't</u> to help everyone, just the <u>poorest people</u>.

We are lifting the shadow of the workhouse from the homes of the poor.

David Lloyd George

The Old Age Pensions Act — an over-70s free for all...

This page looks like a <u>shocker</u> to learn, but there are only <u>a few</u> main points. <u>Children</u> got legal protection, school dinners, medical check-ups and Borstal. <u>Old people</u> got pensions. Make sure you know the <u>dates</u> and <u>names</u> of the acts. Any other little details are a <u>bonus</u>.

Laws Protecting Working People

The Liberals also passed laws to help <u>working people</u>. Get all of these <u>clear</u> in your mind now — they may be boring, but you need to know the <u>name</u> and <u>date</u> of each Act, and <u>what it did</u> to help people.

People injured at work got compensation

<u>The Workmen's Compensation Act</u> was brought in in <u>1906</u>.

Under the new law <u>employers</u> had to pay workers <u>compensation</u> for injuries and diseases — <u>if</u> they had got them as a result of their work.

The act covered <u>6 million workers</u> who hadn't previously had any legal protection.

The National Insurance Act of 1911

In <u>1911</u> Lloyd George introduced the <u>National Insurance Act</u>. Lloyd George got a lot of the ideas for this Act from a <u>similar scheme</u> running in <u>Germany</u>.

The Act came in two parts. Part One's covered here. Part Two's covered opposite.

Part One helped with health insurance

Part One was to help workers pay for <u>health insurance</u>. The insurance was to pay for <u>treatment</u> and provide <u>sick pay</u> when people were too ill to work.

The National Insurance Act said the Government would <u>top up</u> the money that workers paid into insurance schemes.

1) The Act covered workers earning <u>less than £160 per year</u>.

2) <u>Each week</u> workers paid <u>4 old pence</u> out of their wages into a <u>central fund</u>. Employers added <u>3 old pence</u> per week and the Government added another <u>2 old pence</u> per week.

3) Sick pay of <u>10 shillings per week</u> was paid to <u>male</u> workers if they were off work ill for more than <u>four days</u>. This sick pay would be paid for <u>13 weeks</u>. The worker was also entitled to <u>medical attention</u>.

4) Women <u>didn't pay as much</u> in or <u>get as much</u> out, because they <u>didn't earn as much</u> in the first place.

5) Women were paid <u>7s 6d</u> a week <u>sick pay</u>. They also got a one-off <u>maternity grant</u> of <u>30 shillings</u>.

6) <u>Names</u> of workers on the National Insurance scheme were put on a special list known as a <u>doctors' 'panel'</u>. Doctors were <u>paid</u> a sum by the Government for every patient on the panel.

7) The scheme was organised through organisations approved by the Government — *friendly societies*, <u>trade unions</u> and <u>private insurance companies</u>.

8) The scheme caused <u>controversy</u> — Conservatives said the Government had <u>no right</u> to force people to contribute from their wages, and many socialists said there should be <u>higher taxes on rich people</u> to pay for it instead of workers having to contribute. But it was still <u>passed</u>.

friendly society = a kind of insurance company

Workers are getting nine pence for four pence.

David Lloyd George

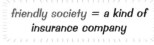

<u>Ten million workers</u> now had health insurance.

Laws Protecting Working People

Here's Part Two of the National Insurance Act, and a couple of other Liberal laws to help workers.

Part Two set up unemployment benefit for a few trades

Part Two of the National Insurance Act provided unemployment benefit for workers in shipbuilding, iron founding and construction. These were industries where workers were quite regularly out of work for several weeks at a time.

It was a contributory scheme. Employers, employees and the Government each paid 2½d per week into an unemployment fund.

...iron foundries and construction...

Shipbuilding...

...but once again nobody's remembered the witches.

Annual General Witchfest 1911

In return workers were paid 7 shillings per week for up to fifteen weeks in any one year if they were unemployed. Payment started from the second week of unemployment.

The Trade Board Act of 1909 set a minimum wage

Winston Churchill and William Beveridge put together the Trade Board Act in 1909 to help sweated industry workers.

Sweated industries included tailoring, lace-making and cardboard-box making. The workers were often women or foreign immigrants who worked from home doing long hours for low wages.

1) The Act set up trade boards for each of the 'sweated industries'.

2) Every board was made up of equal numbers of workers and employers, and a neutral chairman.

3) The board's job was to decide a minimum wage for the industry.

4) Employers paying less than their trade board laid down could be fined.

5) Factory inspectors made sure the Act was put into practice.

By 1914 two million workers were covered by the trade boards and so had the security of a minimum wage.

The Labour Exchanges Act set up job centres

Churchill and Beveridge also worked together on the Labour Exchanges Act. This was passed in 1909 too.

1) Labour exchanges were like job centres. Unemployed workers could go there to find out about job vacancies.

2) Within five years there was a network right across Britain.

3) One million jobs a year were filled through the exchanges.

The Labour Exchange Act — perfect for swapping jobs...

There's a lot of nasty fiddly detail here — don't panic if you can't remember it all. The easiest way to learn the important bits is by making a timeline of acts and dates. Then make sure you can scribble down the main point of each act — who it was meant to help, and what they got.

Effects of the Liberal Reforms

The Liberals' reforms wouldn't do much good if they couldn't <u>pay</u> for them. They had to get the money through <u>taxes</u> — one reason why some people <u>didn't</u> welcome them with <u>open arms</u>.

Lloyd George <u>wanted to</u> raise taxes to pay for the reforms

In <u>1909</u> the Liberal Chancellor of the Exchequer Lloyd George decided he would have to <u>raise taxes</u> to pay for the Reforms. He proposed the tax increases in the <u>1909</u> budget. The budget was designed to tax the rich <u>more heavily</u> than the poor — so it became known as <u>the People's Budget</u>.

- *<u>Income tax</u> would go up from 5 pence to 6 pence in the pound*
- *There'd be a new <u>super tax</u> of 2½ pence in the pound on incomes <u>over £3000</u> per year*
- *The inheritance tax — called <u>death duties</u> — would go up*
- *Tax on tobacco and spirits would go up*

The Liberals had to call a General Election in 1910

To become <u>law</u> the Budget had to be passed by the House of Commons <u>and</u> the House of Lords.

1) Although <u>the Conservatives</u> were <u>bitterly opposed</u> to the Budget, the Liberals got the bill through the <u>Commons</u>. But it was <u>rejected</u> in the House of <u>Lords</u> where Conservatives held the majority.
2) The Liberals <u>couldn't</u> see any way of getting the bill through Parliament. This was a constitutional crisis — the <u>unelected</u> House of Lords was <u>blocking</u> the will of the <u>elected</u> House of Commons.
3) The Liberals called a <u>General Election</u> to make sure they had the British people's support. The <u>only issue</u> of the campaign was the People's Budget.
4) The <u>Liberal Party won</u> the election. They reintroduced the Budget and finally it was passed by the <u>Commons and the Lords</u>.

Vote Lloyd George
He's the best
Helps the poor
And has a hairy chest

To prevent such crises the <u>Parliament Act</u> was passed in <u>1911</u>. The Lords were <u>no longer</u> allowed to reject <u>bills on financial issues</u>. They could reject other bills <u>twice</u> — but the <u>third</u> time it'd <u>automatically</u> become law.

The Liberal Reforms left <u>some problems unsolved...</u>

1) Hardly any of the new schemes were designed to help the <u>whole population</u> — just some people.
2) The <u>National Insurance Act</u> Part One <u>didn't</u> cover the worker's <u>family</u>. Part <u>Two</u> only covered a <u>few</u> industries.
3) The reforms <u>didn't</u> replace the old Poor Law. There were still <u>workhouses</u> — but fewer people in them now.

...but <u>changed attitudes</u> to helping the poor

1) This was the first time that <u>national taxes</u> had been used to help the poor.
2) The State took on <u>responsibility</u> for protecting citizens from <u>extreme hardship</u> in sickness, old age and unemployment for the <u>first time</u>.
3) The schemes were introduced <u>all across the country</u> — they weren't just local affairs.
4) <u>Large numbers</u> of people were covered by some of the schemes — the National Insurance Act Part One covered 10 million workers.
5) There was <u>massive opposition</u> to some of the schemes, but social reform had become a <u>reality</u>.

"The People" 1 — "Peers of the Realm" 0...

The fact that the Liberals had to call a <u>General Election</u> and <u>change the law</u> about the House of Lords shows what a <u>stir</u> they'd caused. The way they <u>changed attitudes</u> is really important too.

Revision Summary

Congratulations if you got through that without feeling a yawn coming on. Parliamentary Acts are only about a microsliver more interesting than watching concrete set — well, that's what I think anyway. When you've had a go at revising each page try answering these questions to see how well you've remembered the facts. If you can't answer them all without sneaking a look back through the section you need to learn the facts again — and again, till you get them all right every time.

1) In 1900 where did old people go when they were really broke?
   a) Workhouse b) Jailhouse c) Schoolhouse d) Outhouse

2) Who ran the workhouses?

3) What are the names of the two men who published reports on poverty in 1901 and 1903?

4) Name three groups of people who thought the Government ought to do more to help the poor.

5) What did most Conservatives think about giving Government help to poor people in 1900? Which other political party agreed with the Conservatives?

6) Which government set up a Royal Commission to look at the Poor Law? What year was it?

7) How many reports did they write? What were they called?
   a) The Liberal and Conservative Reports b) The Majority and Minority Reports
   c) The Little and Large Reports d) The Steptoe and Son Reports

8) Who won the General Election in 1906?

9) What does LEA stand for?

10) Name three things children under 16 weren't allowed to do after the Children's Charter in 1908.

11) What two new ideas did Herbert Samuel come up with to help young offenders?

12) What was David Lloyd George's job when he introduced the Old Age Pensions Act of 1908?

13) What did the Workmen's Compensation Act of 1906 say? How many workers did it cover?

14) How many parts has the National Insurance Act (1911) got?

15) What was Part One of the National Insurance Act about?

16) It's 1912. Thora Runnynose the cotton mill worker has got pneumonia. She earns £90 a year. How much sick pay is she entitled to?

17) It's still 1912. Tommy Tiptoe the miner has been sacked. Will he get unemployment benefit?

18) What's a sweated industry?

19) Which two acts did Winston Churchill and William Beveridge work together on?

20) How many people got a minimum wage by 1914?

21) What was the popular name for Lloyd George's 1909 budget?

22) Who stopped the budget from becoming law first time around?

23) What was the name and date of the act the Liberals brought in to stop this happening again?

24) Give two reasons why these reforms changed attitudes to helping the poor.

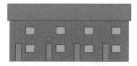

The British Expeditionary Force

BEF stands for British Expeditionary Force. For Britain the First World War began with the BEF going over to Europe to fight the Germans. British people were keen to join up and fight in the war. Nobody imagined it was going to last four years, or take the lives of 3 million Allied soldiers.

Britain declared war on Germany on 4 August 1914

1) Britain was allied to France and Russia by an agreement called the Triple Entente.
2) Germany was allied to the Austro-Hungarian Empire and Italy by an agreement called the Triple Alliance.
3) The Austro-Hungarian Archduke Ferdinand was assassinated by Serbs, in the Bosnian capital Sarajavo on 28 June. Austria-Hungary declared war on Serbia. Russia agreed to help Serbia. Germany declared war on Russia, then on Russia's ally France.
4) Germany already had a strategy for invading France — it was called the Schlieffen Plan.
5) The plan was to push down through Belgium and then capture Paris. According to the Schlieffen Plan the Germans should be able to take control of France within weeks.
6) But Belgium was a neutral country — Britain stepped in to help them and declared war on 4 August.

Britain sent the BEF to help France and Belgium

1) The BEF was made up of 4 divisions of troops. The French Army in the field had 70 divisions.
2) The BEF commander was Sir John French.
3) The British and French aim was to stop the Germans from invading or capturing France.
4) The BEF and the French didn't manage to stop the Germans in Belgium, or to stop them invading France.
5) But once the Germans were in France, the BEF and the French fought three major battles at Ypres (it's pronounced a bit like EEPr), Mons, and the river Marne, which brought the Germans to a standstill.

The German First Army met British forces at Mons on 23 August 1914. The Germans were flummoxed because they didn't expect to see British soldiers. The small British force beat them back — but it wasn't a lasting victory as the French army retreated and the British had to follow.

The Germans needed to cross the Marne to get to Paris. In September 1914, the French managed to beat them back as far as another river called the Aisne. They were supported by the BEF. The German army dug trenches to defend their position. It became clear that the war was going to last longer than a few weeks.

Another German force was coming down through Belgium. They had already captured Antwerp, and were advancing on Ypres. The BEF was sent North to defend Ypres. They fought right through October and November 1914, and managed to hang on to it, but there were terrible casualties. Half the BEF was wounded and 10% killed.

After Ypres the British Army needed more men

1) Kitchener, the Secretary for War, wanted to introduce conscription but Asquith, the Prime Minister, refused.
2) Instead of conscription there was a massive poster campaign — the "Your Country Needs You" one.
3) By September 1914 there were half a million volunteers. Another half million men joined by February 1915.

The ultimate lottery — your country needs you...

Get the order of events in 1914 clear. Remember — the BEF went to help Belgium and France. Write down what happened at Mons, Marne and Ypres from August to November 1914. Learn it.

Trench Warfare

The examiners will want to be really <u>sure</u> you understand what <u>trench warfare</u> is — <u>learn</u> this now...

Trench warfare <u>created</u> <u>deadlock</u>

1) The Generals in charge, including <u>Sir John French</u>, weren't used to <u>this type</u> of fighting. They knew more about the type of battles where everyone met up on a <u>big field</u>, then the cavalry <u>charged in</u>, followed by <u>footsoldiers</u> and backed up with <u>artillery</u>.

2) After <u>Ypres</u> and the <u>Marne</u>, neither side could drive the other back. Both armies <u>dug trenches</u>. By the <u>end of 1914</u> the trenches stretched from the <u>Alps</u> to the <u>North Sea</u>. This line of trenches was called the <u>Western Front</u>.

3) The trenches were <u>easy</u> to <u>defend</u>...   ...and <u>difficult</u> to <u>attack</u>.

> * *machine gun snipers to mow down an attack*
> * *heavy guns behind the trenches*
> * *guards to spot attack from other side*
> * *trenches led back from front line to bring in men and supplies*
> * *protected by barbed wire*

> * *artillery was meant to break through the enemy's barbed wire and wear them down to make attacks easier*
> * *in practice it just warned the other side an attack was coming*
> * *the land between the trenches was often knee-deep or even waist-deep in mud*

4) Even <u>if</u> you made it to the enemy trench in one place, it was hard to <u>hang on</u> to your position because you were <u>surrounded</u> by the enemy's forces in the rest of the trench.

Life in the trenches was <u>hard</u> <u>and</u> <u>dangerous</u>

Each man got paid <u>one shilling</u> a day. The main rations were <u>bully beef</u>, <u>jam</u>, and <u>tea</u>.

Thousands <u>of lives were lost for</u> <u>small gains</u>

1) Both sides had plenty of <u>men</u> and plenty of <u>money</u> for ammunition and weapons, so the Generals kept sending more and more men '<u>over the top</u>' — even though it didn't achieve any <u>obvious</u> success.

2) The major battles in <u>1915</u> were <u>Neuve Chapelle</u>, <u>Loos</u> and the <u>2nd Battle of Ypres</u>. Thousands of lives were lost but neither side <u>gained</u> much from the battles — the front line <u>hardly moved</u> at all.

3) Sir John French was <u>replaced</u> as commander by <u>Sir Douglas Haig</u>.

Trench warfare — wearing the other side down...

You definitely need to know what the trenches were <u>like</u>. The picture will help you. You also need to <u>learn</u> the <u>lists of points</u> (in the blue and red boxes) about attacking and defending the trenches.

Tanks and Aircraft

Tanks and planes were used for the very first time in the First World War. Not surprisingly they made a massive difference to the way wars were fought. That's what you've got to learn about.

At first aircraft were used for surveillance and bombing

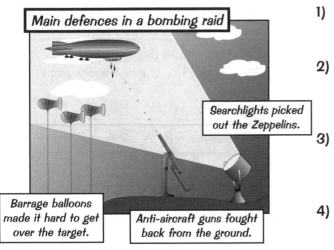

Main defences in a bombing raid

Searchlights picked out the Zeppelins.

Barrage balloons made it hard to get over the target.

Anti-aircraft guns fought back from the ground.

1) On the Western Front both sides used planes and balloons to look for weak points along the trenches where it would be easier to attack.

2) The Germans used hydrogen-filled airships called Zeppelins to carry bombs. In May 1915 there was a major bombing raid on London. The Zeppelins were easy to shoot down because they were so big.

3) Both sides developed planes which could be used for long-distance bombing raids. The first serious raid on Britain was in June 1917 — 95 people were killed at Folkestone. Britain sent bombers into Germany too.

4) By the end of the War, bombers could go hundreds of kilometres without refuelling. The new technology was later used to set up the first passenger airlines.

Fighter planes were developed during the war

1) The early planes were slow and difficult to steer. Also, ordinary machine guns were no use as they were hard to aim, and there was a danger of shooting off the propellors.

2) In 1915 new planes carried synchronised machine guns which wouldn't shoot the propellor. One man could fly and handle the gun — where before they'd always needed two people.

3) The fighter planes were used to escort bombers on raids and to bring down enemy bombers. They also fought each other, especially on the Western Front.

4) The Royal Air Force was formed in 1918 out of the Army's Royal Flying Corps and the Navy's flying units. By the end of the war, the RAF had over 20,000 bombers and fighters.

5) Pilots like Albert Ball and Mike Mannick became national heroes.

Tanks made it easier to attack on the ground

Tank tracks meant they could go over very rough ground, and plough through barbed wire without problems. The heavily armoured body of the tanks meant ordinary gun fire couldn't stop them. Tanks should have allowed the British army to break the deadlock on the trenches, but it took a while to develop effective tactics, and the early tanks often broke down.

1) The first time tanks were used was at the Battle of the Somme in July 1916. Sir Douglas Haig sent in 49 tanks. He could have waited for more, but he decided it was more important to surprise the Germans, and went ahead anyway. The tank division captured 2km of German-held territory but couldn't hold on.

2) At Cambrai on the Western Front in November 1917, tanks were used much more successfully. Nearly 500 tanks advanced about 6km into German territory, but again couldn't hold onto their gains.

New technology — it changed warfare forever...

The development of aeroplanes and tanks as weapons is one of the most important long-term effects of the First World War. Draw a timeline for each weapon, giving dates for the main events.

The Western Front

The Battle of the Somme was a major attack by the British Army against the German line.
It led to a <u>staggering loss of life</u> — and had a <u>long-term effect</u> on how the war was <u>remembered</u>.

The Battle of the Somme killed 1 million men

In <u>February 1916</u>, the Germans began an attack on Allied forces around <u>Verdun</u>.
If they captured Verdun, <u>Paris</u> would be open to attack.

By <u>July</u>, 700 000 men were dead. In order to <u>relieve</u>
<u>the pressure</u> on Verdun, Haig decided on a <u>major attack</u>.

1) This was the <u>Battle of the Somme</u>. It began on <u>1 July 1916</u>.
2) After a massive <u>artillery bombardment</u>, the soldiers were sent
    'over the top' to charge the German trenches.
3) British soldiers were under orders to advance <u>slowly</u>, not run.
4) This gave the Germans time to get ready. The slow-moving British soldiers were an <u>easy target</u>.
5) 57 000 Britons were <u>killed</u> or <u>wounded</u> on the first day alone. 21 000 died in <u>1 hour</u>.
6) The battle dragged on to <u>November</u>. By then over <u>1 million</u> soldiers had died. <u>418 000</u> were British.

The Battle of the Somme had mixed results

1) Despite the <u>months of fighting</u> and all the <u>deaths</u>, very little ground was <u>gained</u>. In <u>some places</u>
    the Allied forces advanced about <u>7 miles</u>, in <u>others</u> it was only a <u>few hundred metres</u>.
2) The Germans <u>weren't beaten</u> at the Somme, but they took a <u>severe battering</u>. The battle probably
    helped to <u>wear them down</u>. This was what Haig wanted — a "<u>war of attrition</u>".
3) Many men in the army were <u>appalled</u> at how many lives were lost. They felt the Generals' tactics were
    <u>wrong</u> — and some started to <u>lose confidence</u> in the officers commanding the war.
4) There was less confidence in the <u>artillery</u> too. They were supposed to <u>destroy</u> the German <u>barbed wire</u>
    before the attack and didn't manage to do it.
5) Back in <u>Britain</u> film footage of the battle was shown in <u>cinemas</u>. Even though some of it was <u>faked</u>
    people were <u>horrified</u> by the reality of the battle. It <u>wasn't</u> the great heroic ideal they'd imagined.

People still can't agree on whether the tactics were right

Many people <u>nowadays</u> feel that the tactics used at the Somme and in other battles were <u>wrong</u>.
Their <u>picture</u> of the First World War comes from <u>TV, books and films</u> — which often see Haig as a "Butcher".
But in fact, it's much <u>more complicated</u> than that. Here are some of the <u>main opinions</u> on <u>both sides</u>.

AGAINST

- *Hundreds of thousands of men were killed under his command. Haig said "The attacks are to be pressed, regardless of loss."*
- *Haig could have waited for more tanks, which might have saved many lives.*
- *Once he saw the first day's slaughter he could have changed his tactics.*

FOR

- *Haig's overall strategy was to wear the Germans down, whatever the cost. It's every general's job to win wars, not to save lives.*
- *Haig couldn't wait for more tanks — he had to relieve the pressure on Verdun, or the whole war might be lost. He used the tanks he had.*
- *By 1918, Haig had learnt to adapt these attacking tactics so that they became highly successful.*

The Somme — be sure to give both sides of the story...

The Somme was a <u>disaster</u> — but many people argue it was <u>necessary</u>. If you're going to write
about it, you have to give <u>both sides</u> of the argument. Don't miss out the actual <u>facts</u> though.

The War at Sea

The First World War didn't <u>stop</u> at the Western Front. The <u>Navy's blockades</u> in the North Sea and the Baltic were really <u>important</u> in wearing Germany down.

Blockades <u>were more</u> <u>important</u> <u>than all-out</u> battles

1) The Royal Navy patrolled the <u>North Sea</u> and the <u>Baltic</u>.
2) The aim was to stop <u>food</u> and <u>supplies</u> for Germany being delivered to <u>German ports</u> or ports belonging to <u>neutral countries</u> like in the <u>Netherlands</u> and <u>Scandinavia</u>.
3) The Navy blockades also <u>prevented</u> German ships from getting out to <u>open sea</u> where they could <u>fight</u>.
4) The <u>only weapon</u> the Germans had against the Royal Navy was the <u>U-boats</u> (submarines). At first Germany was <u>careful</u> not to attack ships from <u>neutral countries</u> or <u>passenger ships</u>.
5) Britain realised this and started <u>shipping arms</u> and <u>ammunition</u> in <u>passenger ships</u>.
6) The British ocean liner the <u>Lusitania</u> was used to bring over <u>weapons</u> in <u>April 1915</u>.
   German U-boats torpedoed the ship and <u>1000 people died</u>, mostly <u>civilians</u>.
7) About 100 of the dead were from the <u>USA</u>. <u>Up to this point</u> the USA was <u>neutral</u>, but <u>after the sinking of the Lusitania</u> America supported the <u>Allies</u>, and <u>joined</u> the war on their side in <u>1917</u>.

The <u>German and British</u> <u>Navies clashed at</u> <u>Jutland</u>

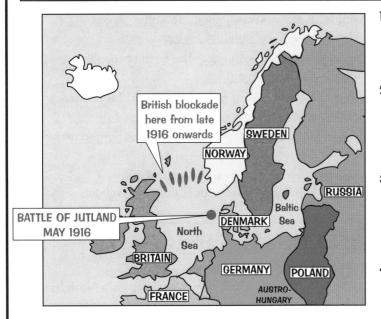

British blockade here from late 1916 onwards

SWEDEN
NORWAY
RUSSIA
Baltic Sea
DENMARK
North Sea
BRITAIN
GERMANY
POLAND
FRANCE
AUSTRO-HUNGARY

BATTLE OF JUTLAND MAY 1916

1) Before the war Germany and England raced to build <u>Dreadnoughts</u> — 18 000 ton battleships. Both sides had <u>invested</u> a lot in the new ships and were <u>nervous</u> of risking them in a big battle.
2) In the end the <u>only</u> major battle between the Dreadnought fleets was <u>The Battle of Jutland</u> in <u>May 1916</u>. Admiral von Scheer hoped to lure the British fleet out of their <u>base</u> at Jutland in Denmark and then unleash a massive <u>attack</u>.
3) The British fleet turned out to be <u>bigger</u> then von Scheer expected and the sides were quite <u>evenly matched</u>. The two sides fired at each other for <u>several hours</u>, but it was a misty evening and hard to see the targets.
4) It's not easy to say which side was the <u>winner</u>:

   - The British lost 14 ships, and the Germans lost 11.
   - The British ships were <u>more severely damaged</u>.
   - The Germans left the battle first.

The Battle of Jutland led to <u>more U-boat attacks</u>

1) <u>After Jutland</u> the German Dreadnoughts stayed <u>in harbour</u>. Britain had <u>control of the surface</u>, but German U-boat attacks on British shipping became <u>more intense</u>.
2) When <u>food supplies</u> in Britain became dangerously low in <u>April 1917</u>, Prime Minister Lloyd George introduced a <u>convoy system</u> which helped ships <u>escape</u> the submarines (see P.15).

The war at sea — blockades, U-boats and Jutland...

The <u>war at sea</u> is a crucial part of understanding how life <u>changed</u> back home in Britain.
The <u>U-Boats</u> threatened <u>food supplies</u> which led to <u>rationing</u>. Make sure you know about <u>Jutland</u>.

Volunteers from the Empire

Don't forget that Britain didn't fight alone in the First World War. As well as the French army, there were also soldiers from the British Empire — from Canada, Australia and New Zealand.

Canadians, Australians and New Zealanders volunteered

1) 418 000 Canadians fought in Europe. Another 200 000 defended Canada. 56 500 died.
2) 322 000 Australian soldiers fought in the First World War. 60 000 died.
3) 124 000 New Zealanders fought in the War. 17 000 died.
4) The Australian and New Zealand Army Corps were known as ANZACs.

Before the First World War Canadians, New Zealanders and Australians still saw themselves as British. They didn't see their countries as separate, so it seemed right to them that they should join up.

Gallipoli was the worst part of the war for the ANZACS

The Gallipoli campaign was fought in 1915 — when the stalemate on the Western Front was at its worst. Britain's main aim was to open up the route to the Black Sea by attacking Turkey, so they could help Russia.

1) The campaign began in February. The Navy tried to advance up the Dardanelles but couldn't get past Turkish forts and mines.
2) The Navy pulled out and the Army was sent in. The force was made up of one British division, and ANZAC and French troops.
3) The idea was to cross the Gallipoli peninsula and capture the Turkish capital Constantinople. The land assault began in April.
4) The Turks were ready for the Allied troops. By firing down from hills above the beaches the Turks stopped the Allies from advancing at all.
5) The ANZACS, French and British were forced to dig trenches. They spent the summer and autumn under fire, suffering from heat and disease, and with poor supplies of food and ammunition. There were 40 000 casualties by August.
6) Perhaps it should have been obvious from the start that the situation was impossible, but it wasn't till December that the evacuation began. 105 000 soldiers were withdrawn.
7) The Turks lost even more men than the allies: 65 000 died. This seriously weakened their army, but it wasn't obvious at the time. In December 1916 it just looked like bad planning.

Over a third of the ANZACs who went to Gallipoli died. Gallipoli is remembered as one of the most wasteful campaigns of the war. Some people argue that it was after Gallipoli that Australia and New Zealand started to see themselves as separate countries.

Canadians served in the Army, the Navy and the Air Force

1) There were 13 000 Canadians in the Air Force, and 3 000 in the Navy.
2) Canadian Army divisions fought on the Western Front. They captured and held Vimy Ridge from the Germans in April 1917. Vimy was a major obstacle to the Germans when they tried an attack in spring 1918.

Gallipoli — another military disaster for the Allies...

Having an Empire made a big difference to Britain in the war. Learn the facts about Gallipoli. Yes, it looks complicated, but it'll look a whole lot better once you've started learning it. Get scribbling.

The War at Home

When the First World War broke out the government had to be sure Britain was ready to cope. They gave themselves special powers by...surprise! getting parliament to pass a law.

Parliament passed the Defence of the Realm Act

The Defence of the Realm Act was passed in August 1914, right at the start of the war. There were two basic things the government was trying to do:

1) Make sure the country had enough resources to fight the war.
2) Make sure British people were in a fit state to fight and support the war effort.

The law allowed the government to...

- introduce conscription

- take control of vital industries like coal mining
- take over three million acres of land and buildings
- bring in British Summer Time for more daylight (working) hours
- control drinking hours and the strength of alcohol

- stop people talking about the war or spreading rumours
- censor newspapers
- enforce rationing

Thousands of men volunteered to fight — but it wasn't enough

When war broke out, thousands of men rushed to volunteer for the fighting. They believed the war would be over quickly — 'by Christmas'. They thought it was going to be an adventure, and wanted to be part of it. The enthusiasm didn't last.

By 1915 the number of casualties was going up — and the number of volunteers was slowing down. On the Western Front so many men were being killed and wounded that there weren't enough volunteers to replace them.

There was also a growing feeling in Britain that it wasn't fair that some men were avoiding military duty.

The Government introduced conscription in 1916

1) All single men aged between 18 and 41 had to fight.
2) When there still weren't enough soldiers married men had to join up too.
3) People who didn't believe in fighting were called conscientious objectors. They were treated as criminals and sent to prison. Some were even shot. They were seen as traitors because they refused to fight.

Women started doing "men's jobs"

I wonder what he's doing now...

Many of the original volunteers came from heavy industries like coal mining. There was a shortage of workers in these industries and without them Britain couldn't supply the army. When conscription started there were even fewer men available to do the vital jobs. Women started taking their places in the pits and factories.

I wonder what she's doing now...

Surviving at home — major changes were needed...

You've got to know all about the Defence of the Realm Act, and conscription — scribble and learn.

Food Shortages

Britain had problems keeping food supplies going in the war. Something needed to be done to make sure nobody starved. The important thing is to learn all three of Lloyd George's tactics.

German U-boats made it hard to import food

In 1914 Britain was used to importing quite a lot of food from the United States and countries that were part of the Empire. Germany used U-boats (submarines) to attack shipping all round Britain and made it impossible to import all the food Britain needed to survive. By April 1917 Britain only had six weeks' supply of wheat.

Britain used blockades against Germany too. There's more about the war at sea on P12.

The Prime Minister was David Lloyd George. He took three big steps to solve the food crisis.

1) Navy convoys protected merchant ships coming in to Britain

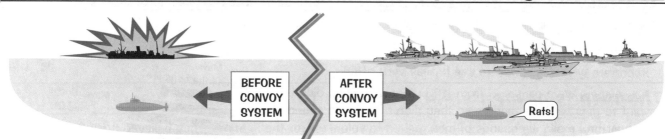

BEFORE CONVOY SYSTEM

AFTER CONVOY SYSTEM

Rats!

Ships travelling alone were easy targets for the U-boats. 25% of merchant ships coming into Britain were being sunk.

The Navy began a convoy system. Merchant ships travelled in groups with an escort of Royal Navy ships to protect them.

U-boats couldn't attack as easily. With the convoy system only 1% of ships were sunk.

2) Food rationing started in 1918

When food rationing started in 1917 it was voluntary. In 1918 shortages were still a problem and rationing was made compulsory for beer, butter, sugar and meat. People still got roughly the same amount to eat. The idea was to control the food supply, not the amount of food people had to eat.

1) Everyone got rationing coupons. They had to hand them over when they bought beer, butter, sugar and meat. When the week's coupons for say, sugar, ran out, they couldn't buy any more that week.

2) Some people hoarded food, partly because they were afraid it would run out, and partly because of increasing prices. They would sell it on later creating a 'black market' in food.

3) There were shortages of some kinds of food but no-one starved.

4) The Government had never been this involved in organising people's daily lives before.

3) Britain grew more food

Farmers were encouraged to use more of their land so they could grow more food. There was an excellent harvest in 1917.

The Women's Land Army was set up. Women from the Land Army were a big new labour force available to work on the farms.

Food supply — crucial to avoiding a crisis...

How Lloyd George avoided a Food Supply Crisis isn't the most exciting topic in this section — but you've definitely got to know about the three steps he took: convoys, rationing and production.

Attitudes to the War in Britain

There's a dramatic difference between people's cheerful attitude at the beginning of the war and their horror at the waste of life by the end. Make sure you know why attitudes had changed so much.

At the start the war looked like an adventure

In 1914 there was huge enthusiasm for the war. It seems strange now, but of course nobody at the time knew what it was going to be like.

These are some of the things people felt about the war:

Fighting in the war would be an adventure.	It was right to fight for your country when it went to war.	The war would be "over by Christmas". Britain would win easily.

Obviously not everybody thought exactly like this — but a fair few did.

At first people didn't really know what was going on

The Government deliberately kept people ignorant of what was going on:

1) Letters from soldiers were censored.
2) Reporters weren't allowed to see battles very often.
3) Newspapers were censored from 1915. Anyway, they didn't want to depress their readers so they didn't let things sound as bad as they really were.
4) No photographs could be taken which showed dead soldiers.
5) Casualty figures weren't available from the Government.
6) Often even Parliament wasn't told how the war was really going.

Dear Mavis,
Me and the boys are having a ███████ time.
███████████████
███████████████
███████████████
Lots of love,
Pete

Mavis Scone
15 Canal St
New Bradwell
Bucks

There had never been a war where most of the fighting was done in trenches before, and there had never been a war where so many people were killed before. People who weren't actually involved in the fighting couldn't begin to imagine how many people were dying, and how awful the trenches were.

During the war ordinary people's attitudes changed

The Government couldn't keep the facts about the War secret forever.
As the war carried on people couldn't help finding out more, and attitudes began to change.

1) During the war 1500 civilians were killed in bombing raids. This was a new and terrible danger.
2) There were no obvious successes on the Western Front up until 1918. There were several disasters, like the Somme and Gallipoli. The deaths seemed pointless when there was nothing to show for them.
3) The Government could hide the overall casualty figures, but they couldn't hide crippled and blinded veterans who returned to Britain, or keep deaths secret from the families of soldiers.
4) Soldiers returning on leave were able to describe the trenches.
5) Many writers and artists celebrated the war at the start. By 1917, many soldiers were disillusioned with the way the war was being run. From then on, and well into the 1920s and 1930s, people wrote poems and autobiographies about how awful life in the trenches had been.
6) Rationing was difficult, and richer people felt it was a hardship. Taxes had increased to pay for the war.

By 1917 most people in Britain were sick of the war, and wanted to see it end.

The First World War — a national disaster?...

OK — this page is about people's opinions and attitudes about what happened, as well as the basic facts. Scribble a list of the main reasons why attitudes to the war changed between 1914 and 1917.

The End of the War

The war changed everybody's lives whether they'd been away <u>fighting</u>, or stayed at home. It wasn't easy to get used to <u>normal life</u> again — especially for the soldiers. Learn all these <u>effects</u> of the war.

The war finally ended in November 1918

1) The USA joined the Allies in <u>April 1917</u>. Only <u>one division</u> was sent at first.
2) More Americans were sent during <u>1918</u>. The German commander <u>Ludendorff</u> decided to try <u>one more</u> big attack <u>before</u> there were so many Allied troops that a German victory would be impossible.
3) The Ludendorff offensive <u>nearly worked</u>, thanks to <u>new tactics</u> in trench warfare — attacking <u>several points</u> along the line at the <u>same time</u>, with a constant artillery bombardment of the enemy as support.
4) The Allies counterattacked from different sides. <u>Haig</u> began an attack on the German line near <u>Amiens</u> in France on <u>8 August 1918</u>. Hundreds of tanks were sent in and the Germans were pushed back through France <u>towards Germany</u>. The Allied forces <u>could have</u> pushed right through into Germany, but <u>before</u> that happened an <u>armistice</u> (a sort of ceasefire) was signed.
5) The trench warfare had <u>worn Germany down</u>. <u>Mutinies</u>, <u>food shortages</u> and <u>revolution</u> in Germany made it <u>impossible</u> for the Germans to carry on. They <u>asked for</u> the armistice and it was signed on <u>11 November</u>.
6) The peace treaty was signed at <u>Versailles</u> in <u>January 1919</u>.

> * Germany had to return land taken from France, Belgium, Poland and others.
> * German colonies in Africa were shared between France and Britain.
> * Germany had to pay reparations of £6600 million to compensate the Allies for the cost of the war.

7) The <u>main negotiators</u> at Versailles were <u>Lloyd George</u>, <u>Clemenceau</u> the French Prime Minister, and <u>Woodrow Wilson</u> the US President. The <u>French</u> thought the peace treaty should <u>punish</u> Germany. Lloyd George thought it was important to punish Germany, but <u>not</u> to make them <u>bitter</u>.
8) The Versailles treaty <u>embittered</u> and nearly <u>bankrupted</u> Germany. It would be remembered in the future.

The war was known as "the war to end all wars"

People in Britain thought there could <u>never</u> be another war as bad as the First World War.
The <u>mood</u> in Britain immediately after the war was pretty <u>bleak</u>.

1) The government had tried to <u>control information</u> during the war. Even so, people had found out some <u>real</u> facts about the war. Many now felt that <u>politicians</u> and <u>authority figures</u> couldn't always be <u>trusted</u>.
2) Many people <u>came to believe</u> that the Generals had been <u>incompetent</u>, and that they <u>didn't care</u> how many lives were lost. This gave people <u>even more reason</u> to stop trusting people in powerful positions.
3) The <u>public school officers</u> in the trenches turned out to be no more competent than the <u>working class soldiers</u>. Some people began to <u>question</u> the way the upper classes dominated society.
4) Soldiers who'd been through the War were even more <u>disillusioned</u> when they returned home. There was <u>unemployment</u> and <u>poverty</u>. They wondered what they had been <u>fighting for</u>.
5) <u>No war</u> in history had produced so many <u>casualties</u>. It felt as though the loss of <u>huge numbers</u> of young men had changed the <u>balance of society</u>.

There were some <u>positive</u> outcomes of the war too. Even though people had many reasons to be <u>disappointed</u> there <u>was</u> a sense of satisfaction that Britain had won. Attitudes towards <u>women</u> and the <u>poorer</u> members of society generally improved, as the war showed <u>everyone</u> could do something useful if they were given the opportunity.

<u>Lloyd George</u> got <u>re-elected</u> as Prime Minister in <u>December 1918</u>.

The Versailles Treaty — the roots of another war...

Don't forget the <u>final facts</u> about <u>1918</u> and the <u>Versailles Treaty</u>, as well as the <u>effects</u> of the war. If you do an <u>essay</u> about the effects of the war, include the <u>positive</u> things as well as the <u>negative</u> ones.

Revision Summary

Phew — a huge section of stuff to learn here. Just keep in mind that you need to concentrate on Britain's role in the war: how life changed at home, and how the reality of war changed people's attitudes to governments, the upper classes and to war. These questions are here to test what you've learnt. They aren't GCSE questions — and they're not what you'll get in your Exam. But they will show you if you've got this topic straight in your own mind... or if you've still got a bit of work to do. It's your choice whether or not you do them — it's your grade in the Exam, after all.

1) Who were Britain's allies at the start of the First World War?

2) What was the Schlieffen Plan? How was it supposed to work?

3) What does BEF stand for? *a) British Exploring Force. b) British Expeditionary Force.*

4) Name the three major battles fought in 1914 which stopped the German advance.

5) How many men had volunteered for the army in Britain by September 1914?

   a) a million b) a quarter of a million c) half a million

6) Give two reasons why trenches were easy to defend.

7) Give two reasons why trenches were easy to attack.

8) Who replaced Sir John French as the British commander in 1915?

9) What two things were aircraft used for during the war?

10) Give two reasons why tanks made ground attacks easier than before?

11) What was the reason for the British attack on the Somme?

12) How many men were killed or wounded on the first day of the Battle of the Somme?

13) Give two reasons why some people say Haig's tactics at the Somme were wrong.

14) Give two reasons why some people say Haig's tactics at the Somme were right.

15) What weapon did the Germans use against the Royal Navy and passenger ships?

16) Give two reasons why it's hard to say who won the Battle of Jutland, 1916.

17) What does ANZAC stand for?

18) What was the name of the campaign to capture Constantinople from the Turks?

19) Give four things the Government was allowed to do by the Defence of the Realm Act 1914?

20) When was conscription introduced?

21) What three steps did Lloyd George take to avoid a food supply crisis?

22) Give three reasons why people's attitudes to the war changed between 1914 and 1918.

23) Give two of the main points from the Versailles Treaty 1919.

24) Give two reasons why the mood was bleak in Britain after the war.

Women's Rights in 1900

Women in 1900 were treated differently from men. Most women didn't go to school or university, and instead spent their lives raising children and working to run a house. Not much of a life...

Women couldn't vote in national elections

During the nineteenth century, several reform acts had given more and more people in Britain the vote — but only men. Most of the population thought it was perfectly sensible that women didn't have the vote.

1) They thought the big wide world was man's business. Women's business was looking after the home.

2) Many people believed that women weren't very rational so they wouldn't be able to make big decisions.

3) Many politicians thought that men needed to be householders to get the vote. Only a very few rich women owned houses or paid the rent, so it would be a bit odd to give them a vote.

4) If only rich women got the vote they'd most likely vote Conservative. The Liberals didn't like that idea.

After 1894 women were allowed to vote for district councils, and to sit on the councils. But they still couldn't vote in national elections for MPs or become MPs themselves.

Women's legal rights weren't equal — but getting better

For a long time married women were not protected in law — but several new laws in the nineteenth century had made things much better. These laws gave them more rights in marriage.

1857   The Matrimonial Clauses Act made it easier for a woman to get a divorce through ordinary law courts. You needed to prove your husband had committed adultery or cruelty or left you. Before the Act, only Parliament could grant divorces.

1870   The Married Women's Property Act gave women the right to keep their property and earnings when they got married. Before the Act it all went to the husband automatically.

       The Married Women's Act said that a husband who left his wife had to keep paying for her maintenance — i.e. her living expenses.

1886   The Guardianship of Infants Act allowed women to be their children's legal guardians if the father died or if the marriage broke up. Being the legal guardian meant having responsibility for any property left to the children as well as seeing they were properly looked after.

They had a chance of an education or a professional job

The North London Collegiate School for Girls was founded by Frances Mary Buss in 1850, and Cheltenham Ladies College was founded by Dorothea Beale in 1858. These fee-paying schools were expensive, and so no use to most women, but they did set a high standard for secondary education for girls.

Girton College at Cambridge University was founded in 1869. Women could go to lectures and have tutorials, though they couldn't get degrees. Most British universities were admitting women by 1900.

Queen's College, London was opened to train women teachers in 1858.

Hiya — I'm Florence.

NURSING IS A PROPER JOB F. Nightingale

MEDICINE
Medical schools opened their doors to women in 1876. The first woman to become a qualified doctor in Britain was Dr. Elizabeth Garrett.

TEACHING
More and more girls' schools opened towards the end of the century providing teaching jobs for women.

NURSING
Florence Nightingale established nursing as a proper job. She set up training schools where women could train to be nurses.

Hmmm — who'd want to be a woman in 1900...

Women's lives in 1900 weren't that great — make sure you learn the reasons why many people thought women shouldn't vote — and the four acts which had given women more legal rights. They'll be handy later.

The Campaign for the Vote 1900–1914

The campaign for women's votes wasn't brand new in 1900 — but the campaigns from 1900 to 1914 were more energetic than ever. Some campaigns were peaceful, some weren't...

The SUFFRAGISTS were moderate in their protests

1) The Suffragists' formal name was the NATIONAL UNION OF WOMEN'S SUFFRAGE SOCIETIES.

2) They were founded in 1897. Their leader was called Millicent Fawcett.

3) Their main tactics were persuasion, meetings and petitions to Parliament.

suffrage = the right to vote

The SUFFRAGETTES were more direct

1) The Suffragettes' formal name was the WOMEN'S SOCIAL AND POLITICAL UNION.

2) The movement was founded by Emmeline Pankhurst in 1903, with her daughters Christabel and Sylvia.

3) The Suffragettes thought the Suffragists took things too slowly. They wanted to see results, and fast.

4) The Suffragettes didn't mind getting arrested. It attracted some sympathy and showed they were serious about getting the vote. In 1905 Christabel Pankhurst and Annie Kenney heckled Sir Edward Grey, who was speaking at a meeting in Manchester, and ended up in prison for a week.

5) They thought the Liberal Government after 1906 would be sympathetic. They were encouraged by the 1907 Qualification of Women Act which let women become county and borough councillors, or mayors.

After 1912 the protests got more extreme

By 1912 the Liberal Government had accepted the idea of some women voting, and tried to put it into their Plural Voting Bill for Parliament to discuss. But the Speaker refused to let them add it. The Suffragettes were furious and protests got far more extreme and violent.

1) Suffragettes chained themselves to railings outside Downing Street and Buckingham Palace.

2) They physically assaulted politicians. The Prime Minister, Asquith, was attacked on a golf course. Suffragettes tried to tear off his clothes, and beat him with dog whips.

3) They destroyed paintings in the National Gallery, and smashed shop windows.

4) Suffragettes made arson attacks on post boxes, churches and railway stations. They even bombed the house of Lloyd George, the Chancellor of the Exchequer.

5) At the 1913 Derby at Epsom, a Suffragette called Emily Davison threw herself under the feet of the King's horse. She died of her injuries. The 1913 Derby was then referred to as The Suffragette Derby.

Suffragists thought these tactics held the campaign back.
They were probably right — the Government didn't want to be seen to be giving in to violence.
The violence also put off many moderate supporters.

The Government dealt with the protests harshly

1) They sent many Suffragettes to prison. The Suffragettes often went on hunger strike, so the prison authorities force-fed them, but this was dangerous and violent.

2) The "Cat and Mouse" Act was passed in 1913. Under this Act the authorities could release hunger strikers then rearrest them when they were fit again.

Women's suffrage — I get the -gist...

Try not to get Suffragettes and Suffragists mixed up. Watch out for questions on whether protests helped win the vote — you'll need to write about all the types of protest, and what effect they had.

Women and the Vote 1918–1928

At the end of the First World War there was a different attitude to the Suffrage Movement. Partly, the war had made the Suffragette violence of 1913 and 1914 seem a bit less serious. But there were other reasons too — especially the work women had done for the war effort.

During the war women did "men's jobs"

1) Basically, so many men were away fighting in the war that there weren't enough to do vital jobs. The jobs were opened up to women — women were happy to take them, and they proved that they could do them just as well as men.

2) Women worked as: bus conductors, drivers, postal workers, farm labourers and coal deliverers. All these vital jobs kept the country going.

3) They also worked in the munitions factories, and engineering workshops. This work was technical, and directly related to the war effort.

4) Women also joined women's branches of the armed forces, and worked as nurses in military hospitals.

By doing work that helped Britain win the war, women proved that they were important to public life as well as home life. There was also a sense of gratitude towards women for their contribution.

The other reasons for giving women the vote were...

1 A shake-up of the voting system was already happening. There was a rule that a man could only vote after living at the same address for 1 year. This needed to be changed to allow soldiers who had been away fighting to vote. If the voting system was going to be changed anyway, it was a chance to include women.

2 People's attitudes to women had changed — and not just because of the war. A lot of people remembered the Suffragettes' protests and felt it was unfair that women had been denied full political rights.

3 The Suffragettes had called off their campaign at the beginning of the war. Nobody wanted them starting up again.

Women 30+ got the vote in 1918

1) The Representation of the People Act was passed in 1918.

2) Not all women got the vote. The ones who did had to be:

over 30 and a householder	OR	married to a householder

The same act gave all men over 21 the right to vote.

3) Women were also able to become MPs. Constance Markiewicz, a Sinn Fein candidate, was elected in 1918 but didn't take up her seat. The first woman to actually become an MP was Nancy Astor who got elected in 1919.

4) The vote didn't go to all women over 21 until 1928, when women finally got equal voting rights.

Voles for women! — sorry, I think I misread that...

The 1918 Representation of the People Act is a big landmark — make sure you know exactly which women got the vote. But just as important, scribble a list of the main reasons why they got it.

Changes in Society & the Law

If you're not doing the special AQA option on women in the twentieth century you can skip the next two pages. If you are doing it you'll need to learn them extra well.

Getting the vote didn't lead to instant equality

1) In general men in 1918 were healthier, better educated and better paid than women. It was also easier for them to get work.

2) Women hoped that when they had the vote they'd be able to get these inequalities sorted out through Parliament.

3) Having laws passed wasn't the only way to make changes though. The attitudes of men and women needed to change too.

You may have the vote my dear, but I still carry more weight in society than you.

1918

There were several changes to the law

Learn this bit first. I know it's boring. I know it's a list of dates. But you have to know it.

1919	The Sex Disqualification Act allowed women to take teaching jobs at universities and become lawyers, magistrates and architects. These jobs had all been closed to women before.
1925	Women were allowed to work in the Civil Service but had to leave if they got married.
1969	The Equal Pay Act said women had to get the same pay for doing the same work as men. Men in the unions had been strongly against this. They thought if women were well-paid it would be harder for the men to argue for a decent wage to support their families with.
1975	The Sex Discrimination Act made it illegal to treat people differently because of their sex. This applied to jobs, getting housing, and almost anything you can think of. One exception was the armed forces (Army, Navy and Air Force), where women can still only do certain jobs.

In time it got easier for women to go out to work

Between the wars (that's 1918-1939) new industries like telephone and radio manufacturing took women on in the factories. There was also more need for clerks, secretaries and typists. Many women took these new jobs.

NB the new jobs were mostly only available in the South and Midlands. Other parts of the country had massive unemployment, so there were no new opportunities for women there. See P.32.

After the First World War women who'd worked in the factories, armed forces or nursing were expected to go back to looking after the home, and let men do the work again. But after the Second World War women who'd gone to work often stayed on in their jobs.

The attitude that "a woman's place is in the home" had softened a bit.

Factories and other work places tried to make it easier for women to come and work for them. They supplied laundries and creches on-site, and offered part-time and shift work so women could fit work in with looking after a family.

Part-time workers have less legal protection than full-time workers. It's easier to pay them less — so many employers weren't just taking women on out of the kindness of their hearts.

Changes in Society & the Law

During the course of the century, a lot of <u>women's lives</u> have been <u>transformed</u> — partly because of new opportunities, and partly because there's <u>more freedom</u> from <u>domestic drudgery</u>. About time...

Women have *fewer kids* and their *health* has *improved*

In <u>1900</u>, most women had <u>no access</u> to contraception. Abortion was <u>illegal</u> — so if they got pregnant they usually <u>had</u> to have the child. The result was that many women were pretty much <u>pregnant all the time</u>.

1) A woman called <u>Dr. Marie Stopes</u> did a lot to make contraception <u>more available</u> to women. She opened <u>family planning clinics</u> all around the country starting in London in <u>1918</u>.

2) The 'pill' was invented in the <u>1950s</u> and became widely available in the <u>1960s</u>. Women now had <u>more control</u> over whether or not they got pregnant, and the <u>size</u> of families <u>dropped</u> as a result. It also meant they could plan a <u>career</u> around children, instead of having to <u>give up work</u> if they had kids.

3) <u>Abortion</u> was made <u>legal</u> for the first time in <u>1967</u>. This gave women the <u>choice</u> to end pregnancies.

4) <u>Fewer pregnancies</u> also means <u>better health</u> — and less risk of dying in childbirth. Better medical care in general means pregnancies are <u>safer</u>, and women can choose to wait till their 30s or 40s to have kids.

Education *for women has* improved

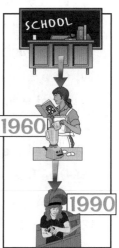

1) Right up to the <u>1960s</u> far <u>fewer women</u> than men went on to <u>university</u>.

2) Overall education for girls <u>wasn't</u> as <u>good</u>. They <u>didn't</u> get to <u>study</u> as <u>many subjects</u> as boys, especially <u>sciences</u> and practical subjects like woodwork. Girls were expected to be more interested in <u>languages</u>, and "home-making" subjects like <u>cooking</u> and <u>sewing</u>.

3) Making girls study "girly" subjects meant they were only educated to do "women's" jobs. <u>Without</u> a decent <u>science education</u> it was <u>pretty hard</u> for women to get into <u>industry</u>, engineering, architecture, medicine, and plenty of other careers.

4) By the end of the <u>1980s</u> the <u>curriculum</u> was <u>basically the same</u> for girls and boys.

5) On average girls now get slightly <u>better results</u> than <u>boys</u> at GCSE, A-level and university.

Running a house *isn't a* full time job *any more*

1) Washing machines, vacuum cleaners, fridges and freezers have now become <u>standard equipment</u> in British homes. They <u>definitely</u> make running a house <u>easier</u> and less <u>time-consuming</u>.

2) In the <u>1950s</u> and <u>1960s</u>, and definitely before then, housework was a <u>full time job</u> for many women.

3) <u>TV advertising</u> began in the <u>1950s</u> and <u>1960s</u>. The first adverts for <u>household appliances</u> were aimed at women, which <u>reinforced the idea</u> that it's women who stay at home and do the cleaning.

There isn't *full equality* yet — but *opportunities* are more *equal*

1) More avenues have <u>opened up</u> to women — including politics. <u>Margaret Thatcher</u> became Britain's <u>first woman Prime Minister</u> in <u>1979</u>. She was <u>hugely admired</u> and <u>respected</u> by many of her <u>male</u> colleagues.

2) The <u>top jobs</u> aren't distributed 50/50 — <u>yet</u> (this is called the 'glass ceiling'). <u>Equality of opportunity</u> only came in <u>relatively recently</u> (in the <u>1980s</u> and <u>1990s</u>). It will take <u>time</u> to <u>filter through</u>.

3) In the <u>1980s</u> and <u>'90s</u>, attitudes to <u>work</u> and <u>claiming benefit</u> changed. Increasingly, <u>everyone</u> was expected to go out to <u>work</u> and <u>contribute</u> to the <u>economy</u>. <u>Stay at home</u> mums were <u>looked down on</u> by some people — especially if they <u>claimed benefits</u>.

Birth control — something to do with New Labour...

Make a list of the main <u>changes to women's lives</u> in the last century — it's what they'll ask about.

Revision Summary

This topic is really about comparing different periods of the twentieth century. Women's rights and freedoms changed pretty drastically during that time, and the best way to see that is to scribble a list of women's rights and freedoms in 1900, and then another list of their rights and freedoms now. It makes scary reading. These questions are here to make sure you've got this section sussed — you know what happened and when. Just start by having a go, then go back over the section and look at the areas you weren't sure about. And then try the questions again.

1) Give four reasons why some people believed women shouldn't have the vote in 1900.

2) What did the Matrimonial Clauses Act of 1857 do to help married women?

3) What two acts were brought in, in 1870? What did they do to help women?

4) Give three possible jobs that a young woman could do in 1900.

5) Name three educational establishments for girls or women.

6) Who were the Suffragists? Who was their leader?

7) Who were the Suffragettes? In what ways were they different from the Suffragists?

8) What happened in 1907 to encourage the Suffragettes?

9) What happened in 1912 to make the Suffragettes' campaign turn more extreme?

10) Give four examples of extreme tactics used by the Suffragettes.

11) What was the reaction of the Suffragists to these tactics?

12) How did the Government deal with these protests?

13) List all the advantages and disadvantages of the Suffragettes' tactics you can think of.

14) Give four reasons why some women got the vote after the First World War.

15) What categories of women got the right to vote in the Representation of the People Act, 1918?

16) When did women finally get equal voting rights to men? What age did they have to be?

17) Name three Acts which changed the law and improved rights for working women.

18) How did the availability of jobs change between the wars?

19) What sort of things did factories and other work places offer to encourage women to come and work for them? Give two reasons for why the factory owners might have done this.

20) How did the wider availability of contraception change women's lives?

21) What were some of the problems in education for girls during the twentieth century?

22) How did housework change during the century?

23) Give two examples of how women have more opportunities now than they did in the 1960s.

24) Give two examples of how women and men were still not treated equally by the end of the twentieth century.

25) Write down three things that have made women's lives better than they were in 1900?

Support for Socialism in 1900

By 1900, many working-class people felt they weren't represented by the established political parties. About this time new organisations were starting to be heard: the Labour Party and the trade unions.

Socialist ideas were more popular than ever

Socialism says that big businesses should be owned by the Government. The fancy term for this is "nationalisation". It also says that society should be organised in a way that deliberately takes care of working-class people as well as the middle and upper classes. Various socialist groups had been set up in the nineteenth century.

1) The Social Democratic Federation was set up by H.M.Hyndman in 1884. It supported socialist reforms. The SDF thought violent revolution was the only way to achieve change. At first it appealed mainly to middle-class people, but became more popular with the working class.

2) The Fabian Society was founded in 1884 too. It was an intellectual group including the writers H.G.Wells and George Bernard Shaw. The Fabians didn't support the idea of revolution. They wanted to spread socialist ideas gradually through elections.

3) James Keir Hardie founded the Scottish Labour Party in 1888. This turned into the Independent Labour Party in 1893, and finally became the Labour Party in 1906.

4) Trade unions were organisations of workers that argued for better pay and working conditions. They had very wide support amongst working-class people. In the 1880s trade unions organised successful strikes by the gasworkers, match girls, and dockers. This gave them added political clout.

More working-class men had the vote

1) The 1884 Reform Act had given the vote to all male householders in towns who paid rates. In the country all men who paid £12 a year in rates (or more) got the vote too.

2) The Ballot Act was passed in 1872. It made voting in general elections secret — so it was harder for corrupt politicians to bully people into voting for them.

3) The 1872 Reform Act gave all male householders the vote.

There were now far more working-class men who had the vote. A party which supported the working-class had a better chance of success than ever.

> Don't forget it was 1918 before all working-class men had the vote.

Working-class men wanted a party that supported their views

1) Working-class people were concerned about problems like unemployment and poverty. (see P.1)

2) The Liberals and Conservatives still largely represented the views of the middle and upper classes. Some working-class voters began to believe that voting Liberal or Conservative was not going to bring a swift end to their problems.

3) All the socialist groups were closer to working class concerns than the Liberals and Conservatives. They needed to combine forces to have any success in a General Election.

Get working — it's the only way you'll learn this...

Three big points about 1900 here: 1) There were lots of groups around with socialist ideas, who wanted to help the working class; 2) Lots more working-class men had the vote; 3) These working class men wanted to use their vote to elect a Government which would improve their lives. It sounds complicated but it isn't.

The Labour Party

This might look like a long list of dates. That's because it is a long list of dates — showing the rise of the Labour Party over the first half of the twentieth century. And yes, it is worth learning.

Labour didn't get into Government till 1924

1888   The Scottish Labour Party was formed by James Keir Hardie.

1892   James Keir Hardy and 2 independent candidates were elected to Parliament with the support of trade unions, the Social Democratic Federation, and the Fabian Society.

1893   The Independent Labour Party was founded at a conference in Bradford, by delegates from trade unions, the Social Democratic Federation, the Fabian Society and the Scottish Labour Party.

> The Independent Labour Party wanted:
> 1)   an eight-hour working day
> 2)   sickness benefits
> 3)   unemployment benefits
> 4)   widow's pensions
> 5)   help for the infirm

ONIONS — BACKING LABOUR ALL THE WAY

1900   The Labour Representation Committee was formed by some unions, the SDF, the Fabians and the ILP. The aim was to find ways to get Labour MPs into Parliament to deal with the practical problems faced by working people in Britain. Ramsay MacDonald was its first secretary.

1906   29 Labour MPs were elected to Parliament. 'Independent' was dropped from the party name.

1909   The Osborne Judgement said that union money could not be used to fund the Labour Party. This was a blow to Labour MPs, who were not usually as rich as Liberal and Conservative MPs, and relied on financial help from the unions so they could take time out from their normal jobs.

1911   For the first time MPs got a salary — of £400 a year. Many more Labour supporters could now think about becoming MPs.

1913   The Trade Union Act said that unions were allowed to raise money to support the Labour party. But only if a majority of members voted to do it, and individuals were allowed to 'contract out' of paying (i.e. choose not to pay if they didn't want to).

1918   57 Labour MPs were elected.

1924   Ramsey MacDonald became the first Labour Prime Minister. The Government was a coalition — Labour was supported in Parliament by the Liberals. The Government only lasted 10 months.

1929   Labour won 288 seats in the General Election. It was now the largest party in Parliament, but didn't have an overall majority — it still needed Liberal support to form a Government.

1945   The first completely Labour Government was elected. Clement Attlee was the Prime Minister.

Labour tended to win support from people who had voted Liberal before.
As Labour became more successful, the Liberal Party was going into a sharp decline.

History revision — a true labour of love...

Wow, what a lot of dates. Twelve to be precise. It looks like loads to learn, but in fact this page is easier to learn than most of the others in this book. It's just a list really — like a list of players in a football team. And if you can name all the players in your favourite team, you can learn this lot.

Build-up to the General Strike 1919–1926

As the Labour Party was growing, so were the trade unions — especially after the First World War. They became much more active in trying to get better pay and conditions by holding strikes.

Unions were in a strong position after the war

During the First World War (1914–1918), the unions cooperated with the Government. Between 1914 and 1918, there were hardly any strikes. Wages in industry were good. Membership of many unions went up. High wages and membership strengthened the unions. After the war there was less pressure to avoid strikes — and disputes over pay began again.

1) The police and railway workers held successful strikes in 1918 and 1919.

2) Total union membership in 1920 was 8 million.

3) Two new unions were founded — the Amalgamated Engineering Union in 1920, and the Transport and General Workers' Union in 1921. Both became extremely large and powerful.

STRONG ONIONS MAKE STRONG SOUP

Trouble in the coal industry led to the General Strike

During the 1920s there were constant disputes between the coal miners and mine owners, over pay and the length of the working day. These disputes eventually led to the General Strike.

1) During the First World War the coal industry was nationalized — the Government took over ownership and control of the mines.

2) In 1919 a Royal Commission was appointed to decide whether or not to return the mines to private ownership. The Commission recommended that the Government should keep the coal mines. Lloyd George's coalition Government wasn't keen and returned the mines to private ownership in 1921.

3) People were beginning to use gas, oil and electricity more than coal. Also mines in Germany and Poland were using efficient modern machinery, which produced more coal more quickly and more cheaply. The British mines still relied mainly on digging with picks and shovels. Customers couldn't afford British coal, and the mines became less and less profitable.

4) The new private owners announced a cut in wages and longer working hours for the miners. The miners refused to accept this and went on strike. Neither side was flexible or ready to negotiate.

5) The miners union was in a Triple Alliance with the transport workers and railwaymen. When they went on strike they asked for support from these allies. The transport workers and railwaymen thought the miners should have tried harder to negotiate, and refused to join in with the strike on 21st April 1921. This day became known as 'Black Friday'.

6) The miners carried on with their strike even without the support of the Triple Alliance. The strike was a failure as eventually they had to go back to work and accept the pay cut and longer working day.

7) In 1925 coal sales dropped off again. Mine owners announced more wage cuts and longer working days.

8) The miners began negotiations, backed by the Trades Union Congress — a sort of union of all the unions.

9) On 'Red Friday' in June 1925, the government agreed to pay a subsidy to keep miners' wages at the same level. The subsidy would be paid for nine months.

10) At the same time a Royal Commission — the Samuel Commission — looked into what could be done to sort out the dispute. The Samuel Commission reported in April 1926.

The minors strike — toddlers on the rampage...

OK, I admit it — this is the most boring page in the book. You can get away with a sketchy knowledge of the coal disputes, but not too sketchy. You'll definitely need to know why the coal industry was doing badly and what year the Samuel Commission was appointed.

The General Strike 1926

The General Strike was one of the biggest showdowns between the people and Government in the twentieth century — that's one reason why many historians get excited about it. I'm not saying you have to get excited, but knowing exactly what happened might just help you pass your exams.

The Samuel Report was fair but nobody liked it

The Samuel Commission said mine owners should reorganise their businesses and introduce modern machinery. That way the mines would be more efficient and profitable. There would be no need to cut wages and increase hours. This suited the miners but not the mine owners.

The Commission also said the subsidy should stop. Miners would have to take a temporary pay cut until the owners had had time to reorganise the mines. The miners weren't at all pleased with this.

The General Strike began when the subsidy ended

1) Neither side accepted the Samuel Report. The mine owners said they would cut wages on 30 April. The miners said they'd strike on 1 May. The owners locked out the workers on 30 April — starting a strike.

2) The TUC felt that if the miners' wages were reduced, then those of other workers would soon follow. They threatened a strike of all key workers — a General Strike — starting on 3 May.

3) Negotiations between the TUC and the government began on 2 May.

4) But the Prime Minister, Stanley Baldwin, pulled out of the negotiations.

5) In the early hours of 3 May the TUC went to Downing Street to talk again, but Baldwin had gone to bed.

6) The strike began at one minute after midnight on 4 May 1926.

The strikers couldn't close the country down

Thousands of workers joined in with the Strike. There were workers from mining, transport, the railways, construction, shipbuilding, printing, electricity and the steel industry.

1) The printers' strike closed down ordinary newspapers, but the TUC and the Government each produced their own. The Government paper was called the British Gazette, edited by Winston Churchill. It described the strike as violent, disorganised and an attack on the British constitution.

   The TUC's paper, the British Worker, emphasised the solidarity of the strike, and said the strike was an industrial issue, not an attack on the Government. It also attacked Churchill.

2) 30 000 men volunteered for the Organisation for the Maintenance of Supplies. They were mainly students and middle-class men. They kept the buses, trains and London Underground moving.

3) Food supplies were transported in armoured convoys escorted by special constables. In London, Hyde Park was used as a centre for distributing milk. There were no shortages because of the strike.

4) Although the Government expected violence, it wasn't that bad. Some buses were attacked in London, and there was minor crowd trouble in Nottingham, Leeds, Edinburgh, Glasgow and Aberdeen. American newspapers wrote about how peaceful the Strike was — even minor American strikes were more violent.

The Government refused to negotiate, but offered a peace plan drawn up by Sir Herbert Samuel. The TUC called off the strike on 12 May, and everyone except the miners gave up.

Stanley Baldwin said the end of the strike was "a victory for common sense".
The King sent a telegram to the nation asking people not to bear grudges now the strike was over.

Effects of the General Strike

The General Strike is a bit of an odd event — observers from Russia hoped there would be a Communist Revolution, but couldn't believe how peaceful it was. But it had major effects long-term.

The General Strike didn't last long

The General Strike lasted just nine days before the TUC gave in.
There's more than one possible reason (don't you just love history?).

9 days later...

1) The Government refused to negotiate. They saw the Strike as a test of their strength. The TUC realised that the Government was never going to back down, so there was no point in carrying on.

2) The Government's reaction was so strong that there was a danger of violence if the Strike continued — amongst others, Churchill had said "we are at war", and called for armoured cars to protect food convoys.

3) The TUC wasn't keen on the idea of a strike, and weren't well enough organised.

4) The National Sailors' Union and the Firemen's Union didn't want to strike. They went to court to prove they didn't have to. The court said the strike was illegal on 11 May. This took away popular support.

5) Some unions didn't have enough cash to fund their members for long, and the banks wouldn't give them overdrafts. The TUC had already spent £4 million out of their Strike fund of £12.5 million.

6) The TUC thought it would be better to have a definite end to the Strike than for it to fizzle out.

7) There were rumours that the Government was going to arrest the leaders of the TUC and seize their funds.

8) The Labour Party didn't support the Strike — its leader Ramsay MacDonald felt it would lose them votes.

The Strike's failure was a blow to the unions

Ouch — that hurt!
We're the unions you know.

1) The miners stayed out on strike for another six months. When they finally gave in and went back to work they had to accept lower wages and longer hours. The Strike hadn't really improved anything.

2) Some miners and railwaymen who'd been on strike were given a hard time at work. But many business owners became more reasonable to their workers.

3) The Trades Disputes Act was passed in 1927. The Act made it illegal for a union to join a general strike or a sympathy strike (one where you go on strike to support workers from a different union). 'Contracting out' was changed to 'contracting in' (see P.26). In other words, if you wanted to pay towards the Labour Party funds you had to sign a form agreeing to it. More people contracted out so the Labour Party had a drop in income.

4) The Strike cost the TUC about £4 million. Without funds in the bank they weren't in a position to threaten new strikes. Membership dropped to about 4 million by 1933, so the unions had less and less income.

5) There was also a general blow to morale. The unions lost confidence and there were very few strikes right through the thirties.

6) But many workers began to realise that the Labour Party was their best hope of changing the system — and in 1929 Labour won the General Election.

Learn it in general — and then in detail...

The 1926 General Strike is dead important. Scribble a quick date list for these two pages to check you've got all the events straight, then learn the effects of the strike on the unions and Labour.

Revision Summary

Labour and the General Strike — you've seen the film, you've bought the T-shirt, you've read the section, but have you done the revision... Use these questions to test how well you know your stuff — if you can't answer all the questions without looking at the section, you need to go back and get learning.

1) What does "nationalisation" mean?

2) Which socialist group founded in 1884 supported change through violent revolution?

3) Who did the 1872 Reform Act give the vote to?

4) Did the Liberals and Conservatives mainly represent the views of:
   a) socialists b) the working class c) the upper and middle classes?

5) Who set up the Scottish Labour Party?

6) Name the four groups that sent delegates to the Independent Labour Party conference in Bradford in 1893.

7) What five things did the Independent Labour Party want to achieve?

8) In which year did MPs first get a salary? How much was it?

9) What's the name of the first Labour Party Prime Minister?

10) How many people belonged to trade unions in 1920?

11) Name the two big new unions set up in 1920 and 1921.

12) What did the Royal Commission say the Government should do with the coal mines in 1919?

13) Why did British mines have trouble selling their coal during the 1920s? Give three reasons.

14) What was the Samuel Commission's job?

15) What did the miners like about the Samuel Commission report?

16) What didn't the miners like about the Samuel Commission report?

17) Where was Stanley Baldwin when the TUC went to 10 Downing Street on 3 May?

18) What kind of people joined the Organisation for the Maintenance of Supplies?

19) What did the miners do when the TUC called off the General Strike on 12 May 1926?

20) Give three <u>possible</u> reasons why the General Strike didn't last very long.

21) Did the miners get better wages after the General Strike?

22) What sort of strikes were made illegal in the Trades Disputes Act of 1927?

23) What effect did the General Strike have on many workers that may have led to Labour winning the 1929 General Election?

SHINIER MEDALS! BIGGER GUNS!

I was thinking more of decent wages, actually.

The Depression

In an economic depression, business just isn't working. Nobody can make a profit, and there's unemployment and bankruptcy left, right and centre. The Depression in the 1930s was the worst of the century. It started in America, and affected the whole world.

The Wall Street Crash in 1929 started the Depression

1) The US stockmarket crashed in October 1929. Millions of dollars were lost, factories closed, and millions of Americans lost their jobs.
2) Britain and other countries felt the effects. Because US customers had no money to spend, industry worldwide was short of customers. The USA stopped lending money abroad and wanted all loans repaid.
3) Industry couldn't employ people if there was no money to pay them with. One of the worst effects of the Depression was the massive unemployment. By 1931 there were almost 3 million unemployed in Britain.

There are two main reasons why the effects of the Wall Street Crash were bad in Britain:

1) The First World War had drained Britain's resources

1) The huge number of soldiers coming back from the war meant unemployment rose. During the 1920s an economic slump caused a steady rise in unemployment before the crash.
2) The coal mines, railways and other industries had been so busy during the war that there was no time for repairs or improvements. They weren't as efficient as they should have been.
3) Very few houses were built during the First World War. The population was increasing so there was a housing shortage — the poorest people were forced to live in sub-standard housing.
4) Some products were mainly sold abroad before the War. When customers couldn't trade with Britain during the war they found new suppliers, and British industry lost custom.
5) As the economic slump after the war got worse, the Government found itself paying more and more unemployment benefit — but fewer people were contributing to the scheme and it couldn't cope.

2) Britain's staple industries were outdated

Before and during the First World War, the USA and Germany developed new industries like chemical production. Britain didn't, and in 1929 Britain's economy still relied on the same industries as in the nineteenth century: cotton production, steel production, shipbuilding, and coal mining.

Cotton
- The cotton industry lost customers because of the war.
- The mills were out-dated, so it was hard to compete with manufacturers abroad.
- Man-made fibres, e.g. rayon were invented which competed with cotton.

Shipbuilding & steel
- World trade slumped — so fewer goods needed transporting, and fewer ships needed to be built.
- If fewer ships were being built less steel was needed too.

Coal
- Ships now ran on fuel oil not coal.
- British coal was expensive. The stuff near the surface had been dug out and the mines didn't have modern machinery, so it took longer to get the coal to the surface.
- Strikes meant coal production was unreliable so more customers were lost.
- Homes in Britain were switching to gas and electricity and needed less coal.

The Wall Street Crash — a big money accident...

Make sure you learn the two reasons why the effects of the Wall Street Crash were bad in Britain.

Two Britains

Don't go on and on about how grim life was in the 1930s without mentioning that it wasn't the same everywhere. You've got to try and give a balanced view that covers all the facts.

Scotland, Wales and the North of England suffered worst

Traditional industries like cotton production, steel production, shipbuilding and coalmining were based in Scotland, Northern England, South Wales and Northern Ireland. Unemployment and poverty were worst here as these industries were going downhill.

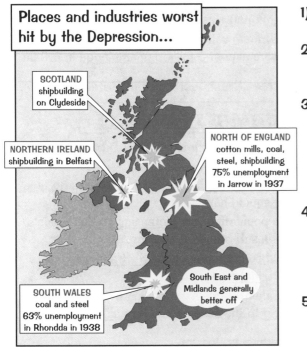

Places and industries worst hit by the Depression...

SCOTLAND
shipbuilding on Clydeside

NORTHERN IRELAND
shipbuilding in Belfast

NORTH OF ENGLAND
cotton mills, coal, steel, shipbuilding
75% unemployment in Jarrow in 1937

South East and Midlands generally better off

SOUTH WALES
coal and steel
63% unemployment in Rhondda in 1938

1) In these areas unemployment hit hard. There were many people living 'on the dole' all through the 1930s.

2) People living 'on the dole' (on benefits) could only afford very basic housing and food. New clothes and shoes were luxuries.

3) There were social clubs in some towns, and allotments where unemployed people could grow their own vegetables, but these were hardly enough to cancel out the dissatisfaction of having no job to go to. The psychological damage to many people from the boredom, frustration and insecurity was huge.

4) The Special Areas Act was passed in 1934 to give extra help to South Wales, Tyneside, West Cumberland, and Scotland. The Act allowed the Government to invest in projects that would bring employment to these areas. e.g. a new steelworks at Ebbw Vale in South Wales.

5) But these areas remained depressed despite any help. BY 1937, there was 75% unemployment in the town of Jarrow.

The Midlands and South East of England still did OK

Meanwhile living standards in the Midlands and South East actually improved during the 1930s. Once the initial economic crisis passed, these areas came out of depression into prosperity.

1) New industries created new jobs in these areas. Power stations for electricity, and factories producing chemicals, cars and aeroplanes were set up in the South East and Midlands.

2) Wages were soon going up faster than prices. The 'average' worker was probably about a third better off in 1939 than in 1914.

3) Quite a lot of new housing was built by local councils during the 1930s. There were still some slums, but the average standard for housing improved.

4) Food imported from the Dominions — Canada, Australia and New Zealand — was cheap for the better paid Southern workers. This meant they had more money to spend on luxury goods or holidays.

5) Now people could afford new inventions like vacuum cleaners, which made housekeeping much easier. This gave them more leisure time — if they also had money they could go on holidays or to the cinema.

6) Taxes were low — people took most of their money home, and could afford these new leisure activities.

Boom and depression — at the same time...

It's really important to know how Britain effectively had two economies in the 1930s — a poor one in the North and Wales, and a booming one in the South and Midlands. Get the reasons clear too.

Government Measures

Politicians and economists were full of ideas about how to tackle the Depression. The two main jobs were to help the unemployed, and encourage British industry.

The dole was the main help for unemployed families

In 1929 an unemployed man could claim for dole. He would get a bit more if he was married, and another small sum for each child in the family. To get the dole, a man had to do two things:

1) *He had to prove that he was actively looking for work. In some areas like South Wales this was a bit of a joke, as there weren't any jobs at all. Even so, he had to keep looking.*

2) *His family had to show it needed the extra money from the dole. This was called a Means Test — it tested if the family had the means to live without the dole. It was designed to make sure taxpayers' money wasn't wasted. If the family had any savings or extra cash — say from a child's Saturday job — the amount of dole money was reduced or even refused completely. The Test was massively unpopular.*

In 1931 over 2.6 million people were unemployed. The National Government couldn't afford all the payments and had to cut the dole by 10%. At the same time they raised income tax.

1) In 1934 the economy began a slight recovery. The Government had more money, and dole went back up to the pre-1931 level.

2) There were also efforts aimed at getting people back to work. In 1936 The Unemployment Assistance Board took over organising the dole and Means Tests, labour exchanges (job centres) and training schemes to help people learn skills which would get them jobs in different parts of the country.

The Import Duties Act of 1932 helped British industry

1) The Import Duties Act was passed in 1932.
2) The Act put a flat-rate tax of 10% on imports coming from outside the Empire.
3) This made goods coming from abroad more expensive than British goods and increased sales of British products. The idea was that industry would pick up again and new jobs would be created for the unemployed.
4) This 10% tax also gave the Government a valuable new income. It meant they didn't have to raise income tax again.

British BARGAIN ONLY £1 000

American car £1 100

The Depression began to lift in the mid-30s

1) *Employment figures began to improve*
Unemployment figures dropped under 2 million in 1936 — and kept dropping. Bank interest rates were very low — property developers and local councils took advantage of this to build new houses and roads, so there were increasing numbers of jobs in construction.

2) *The USA and other countries began to recover*
...and when other economies improved, Britain's economy improved as well. Healthy economies abroad meant plenty of customers for British industry.

3) *The Second World War ended the Depression*
From 1936 onwards the Government started building up arms, because of concerns that there could be another war. This created jobs in the arms factories. When the war actually came there was even more work to be done. There was still some unemployment — but only about 300 000 people by 1941, compared to almost 3 million in 1931.

The Means Test — it sounds pretty miserly to me...

Make sure you know about the Means Test, and the reasons for the lifting of the Depression.

The Reaction to Poverty

The Government's way of solving problems was to think up and pass laws. But ordinary people reacted in all sorts of ways. It's important stuff this — for someone living at the time it would have seemed a lot more real than news about MPs in the Commons discussing a new bill.

Writers described the problems poor people faced

Several authors wrote about the poverty British people were suffering, and the lives they led. They're useful sources for information and opinions written at the time.

1) JB Priestley brought out a book called *English Journey* in 1934. It was a kind of travel book describing living conditions around the country.

2) *The Road to Wigan Pier*, by George Orwell was published in 1937. It was about an area of Lancashire where men traditionally worked in the coalmines, and women worked in the cotton mills. The Depression put everyone out of work in areas like this.

You can't exactly get out a ruler and measure how much books change attitudes, but it's likely that these books made people think about the problems in Britain more than they had before.

There were some protests — without success

1) During the Depression, people in many other countries turned to revolution or parties with extreme political views to solve their problems — like the Nazi Party in Germany.

2) But in Britain, after the General Strike failed in 1926 (see P.28), many working class organisations like the trade unions lost confidence in protest as a way of achieving change.

3) Laws were passed which weakened the unions, and limited their influence on employers.

4) Trade unions concentrated on helping members who were in work.

5) Jarrow was a ship-building town on Tyneside, which suffered terribly from unemployment and poverty in the 30s. In October 1936 200 unemployed ship-workers walked 300 miles to London to protest about the shipyard being closed.

6) This was known as the Jarrow Crusade — but the Government refused to be influenced by it. When the protesters returned to Jarrow they found their unemployment benefit wasn't paid while they were away — because they weren't available for work.

7) The Jarrow Crusade and other marches like it didn't bring any benefits — but it did make many people aware of how bad the situation was amongst the unemployed.

8) One extreme party appeared in Britain — the British Union of Fascists, led by Oswald Mosley. They wanted to set up a Fascist state in Britain — and blamed the Jews for Britain's problems. By 1934 the BUF had 20 000 members and held rallies and fought with other political groups. As the dangers of Fascism in Germany became clearer after 1937, BUF support dwindled.

The Depression changed attitudes to poverty

People who'd lived through the 1930s didn't want to see anything like it in Britain ever again. During and immediately after the Second World War (1939–1945) there was a complete rethink about what help the Government should give people. For more on this, see *Section Seven — The Welfare State*.

The Depression ended — but it had long-term effects...

One long-term effect of the Depression was a big change in attitudes to poverty. But you need to make sure you know about attitudes at the time too — from writers, and protests like Jarrow.

Revision Summary

A nice short section to revise here — but it's worth making sure you've got everything absolutely clear. These questions aren't your typical Exam questions — they're a checklist of the main facts you really do need to know if you've got any hope of doing well. Knowing some of them isn't enough — you should be able to answer the whole lot straight off. If you get the facts clear now, you'll find the Exams a heck of a lot easier.

1) What happens in an economic depression?

    a) Most businesses don't feel any effect at all — just the inefficient ones.

    b) Business isn't working and this leads to unemployment and bankruptcy.

    c) Lots of economists feel sad.

2) What year did the Wall Street Crash happen?

3) Give three examples of how the First World War had drained Britain's resources.

4) Give two examples of how Britain's traditional industries had become out-dated.

5) In which areas of Britain were the effects of the Depression worst?

6) In which areas of Britain was there an improvement in living standards during the 1930s?

7) Give two reasons why some areas of Britain came out of depression into prosperity.

8) What two things did an unemployed man have to do in 1929 to claim for the dole?

9) What was the Means Test?

10) Why was the Means Test unpopular?

11) What did the Unemployment Assistance board take over organising in 1936?

12) Name two effects of the Import Duties Act of 1932?

13) What did property developers and local councils do to take advantage of low Bank interest rates?

14) What effect did the Government's building up of arms after 1936 have on unemployment?

15) Name one writer who wrote about the poverty in Britain during the 1930s.

16) What was the Jarrow Crusade? Did it have any effect on the Government?

17) Who were the BUF?

18) Name one long-term effect of the Depression.

The Outbreak of World War Two

This section's all about <u>Britain</u> during the Second World War. It doesn't cover a lot of important stuff like the <u>Holocaust</u>, and what countries like <u>Russia</u>, <u>Italy</u> and the <u>USA</u> were up to. If you need to know about the rest of the war, you could have a look at the CGP Modern World History book.

Hitler became Chancellor of Germany in <u>1933</u>. During the <u>1930s</u>, he rearmed Germany and started to <u>take territory from other countries</u>. War between Britain and Germany nearly broke out in <u>1938</u> when Hitler's armies invaded <u>Czechoslovakia</u>. The tension came to a head again in <u>1939</u> when Hitler invaded Britain's ally <u>Poland</u>. Britain declared war on <u>3rd September 1939</u>.

The Government and civilians got ready for war

There were no celebrations in <u>1939</u> at the start of the war — people were too <u>worried</u>. The Government took <u>emergency powers</u> — as in the First World War. They had <u>already begun</u> preparing for air raids against civilians in <u>1938</u>, and now took several <u>new steps</u>.

GAS MASKS
Gas masks were first handed out in <u>1938</u> — people were pretty sure there was a war on the way.

AIR RAID SHELTERS
The Government gave away about <u>3 million</u> air raid shelters. <u>Anderson</u> shelters could be buried in the garden, and <u>Morrison</u> shelters were wire cages kept under the kitchen table. There were also public shelters in big towns. In London people used the Underground too.

BLACKOUT
Everybody had to put up heavy curtains or shutters to block the light from their windows. Street lights were dimmed too. The idea was to make it harder for <u>bombers</u> on night-time raids to spot towns and cities.

Ow, that's my ear.

Oops, sorry.

VOLUNTEERS
Volunteers could join the <u>Air Raid Wardens</u> or the <u>Auxiliary Fire Service</u>. They were trained in Air Raid Precautions. The ARP dealt with stuff like early warning of raids, getting people into shelters, putting out fires, and rescuing people from bombed houses.

EVACUATION
1 500 000 children, mothers and babies from industrial and built-up areas, were sent to live in the <u>countryside</u> — away from the danger of bombing raids. They were <u>all moved</u> within 3 days — <u>1, 2 and 3 September 1939</u>.

There weren't any serious air raids in <u>1939</u>. About half the evacuees went home for Christmas in <u>1939</u> — and then returned to the country in <u>1940</u> when the 'Phoney War' (see P.37) ended and the raids got bad.

Germans, Italians and Austrians were put in camps

1) Anyone with a German, Austrian or Italian background was <u>interned</u> at the outbreak of war. That included a lot of <u>Jewish refugees</u> who had come to Britain to escape Hitler.
2) <u>Internment</u> means being put in <u>prison camps</u>. About <u>8000</u> people were held overall — including children. 5000 of them were sent to the <u>Isle of Man</u>.
3) Most people were allowed to go once their <u>backgrounds</u> had been checked out, but some were held <u>all through the war</u>. The Government was worried they might be <u>spies</u>.
4) The internees were held in ordinary houses fenced off with <u>barbed wire</u> and guarded by <u>soldiers</u>.

The 'Phoney' war — six months of waiting and preparing...

People were worried about <u>air raids</u>, and they were worried about <u>spies</u>. Not surprising really. Learn all <u>five</u> preparations for air raids, and what happened to the <u>interns</u> from enemy countries.

Fighting in Europe 1939-40

While the Government at home tried to get Britain ready for war, the British Expeditionary Force waited in France...and waited. Poland had fallen quickly, but the Germans were waiting too.

Hitler invaded Poland — but then nothing happened...

1) Hitler attacked Poland on 1 September 1939. Britain and France were Poland's allies. The invasion of Poland helped bring them into the war.

2) Hitler's invasion was fast and effective. The Polish army was brave and determined but didn't have much modern equipment — they had to send in cavalry to fight Hitler's tanks.

3) By the time Britain and France were ready for war it was too late to help Poland.

> September 1939 to April 1940 is called the
> Phoney War. France and Britain were waiting
> for Hitler's next move — and he was waiting
> to see if they would make peace.

The Phoney War ended in spring 1940

1) By spring 1940 it was obvious to Hitler that Britain and France weren't going to give up just yet.

2) In April Germany invaded Denmark and Norway. A British force failed to help the Norwegians hold the Germans back.

3) The British Prime Minister Neville Chamberlain was forced to resign, and was replaced by Winston Churchill.

4) On May 10th German forces swept through Holland, Belgium and Luxembourg towards France.

5) French and British forces waiting for the German attack realised they would be cut off, and had to retreat. They were chased by the German army, fighting as they went. Finally they were trapped on the beaches at Dunkirk, waiting to be rescued.

As German forces pushed forward British forces had to pull back...

British and French troops had to be evacuated from Dunkirk

A fleet of ships crossed the English Channel to rescue the troops. There were too many men, and not enough Navy ships to carry out the rescue, so civilian fishing boats and pleasure boats were used too. Between May 28th and June 6th 200 000 British and 140 000 French soldiers were evacuated from the beaches in Operation Dynamo. These were the main results.

1) Most of the Army's equipment was left behind on the beach, so there was no way Britain could help France launch a counter-attack against Germany for the moment. Much of France was now conquered.

2) France surrendered to Hitler. Germany now controlled Europe. Britain was now under threat of invasion.

3) Britain needed to replace the men and arms lost at Dunkirk, and prepare for the likely invasion.

4) Churchill made people in Britain feel as though Dunkirk was a victory by concentrating on the bravery of the civilians who'd come to help with the rescue, and the fact that so many men escaped with their lives.

Operation Dynamo — a shining light in the darkness...

In April and June 1940 the Germans caught everyone by surprise. It's important to remember how quickly it all happened — and the main results of Dunkirk. Scribble a list and get it learnt pronto.

The Battle of Britain & The Blitz

Britain was fighting for its life in the summer of 1940 — the German forces were preparing to invade and only the Royal Air Force could stop them. The Battle of Britain was underway.

Hitler sent the Luftwaffe to clear the way for invasion

1) The German plan to invade Britain was called Operation Sealion.
2) The Germans needed control of the Channel to be able to bring troops across to Britain. But these troops would be easy targets for the RAF to attack. So the first part of Operation Sealion needed the Luftwaffe (German air-force) to destroy the RAF, by bombing all its airbases and destroying its planes.
3) The attack on the RAF began in August 1940.

The Luftwaffe failed in the Battle of Britain

By October 1940 the Battle of Britain was over. Here's why:

1) The RAF's pilots were highly trained, skilful and committed.
2) The RAF didn't commit all its planes at the same time — it would have been too risky. This meant they always kept some in reserve — with pilots working different shifts.
3) The RAF were fighting closer to their bases, so their fuel supplies lasted longer.
4) British factories were able to replace planes more quickly than the Germans were.
5) Britain had radar — a new and secret invention — to warn them of German air attacks.
6) By September it was clear that the Luftwaffe hadn't destroyed the RAF.
7) Hitler decided to change tactics — just when the RAF were starting to weaken.
8) The Luftwaffe wasn't actually beaten, but the Government presented the Battle of Britain as a big victory.

What ho! Jerry won't stand a chance against moustaches like ours!

The Blitz began in 1940 and went on till 1941

1) Hitler decided to postpone the invasion of Britain. It was now the only country actively fighting Germany. He hoped to force the British Government into making peace with a new tactic — the Blitz.
2) The Blitz was intense bombing of British cities. It was meant to break the morale of British civilians.
3) The main target cities were London, Birmingham, Bristol, Liverpool, Southampton, Sheffield, Cardiff, Hull, Plymouth, Belfast, Glasgow and Coventry. Each city had either factories, shipyards or naval bases.
4) People living in most other towns, and in the countryside were hardly affected by the Blitz.
5) At first the raids happened in daylight. But Germany lost so many bombers they had to bomb at night.
6) Radar and air raid sirens gave people warning of most raids so they had time to get into the shelters.
7) To keep people's hopes up, Government news films and press releases talked about the bravery and fighting spirit of the civilians. Reports were censored if they gave numbers or photographs of the dead.
8) Bombing carried on throughout the war, but the really heavy bombing of the Blitz ended in May 1941. Hitler realised Britain wasn't going to make peace, and needed the bombers for an invasion of the USSR.
9) During the war as a whole German bombing killed about 60 000 British civilians. But British and American bombing raids on Germany in 1944 and 1945 were much more severe. About 600 000 German civilians died, and 50 000 of them died in just one night during a raid on Dresden.
10) It's worth remembering that even in the worst of the Blitz normal life went on. People still worked, went to school, played football and got on with daily routine. The war didn't bring all ordinary life to a halt.

The Battle of Britain — a real victory...for propaganda...

Hitler's reasons for starting the Battle of Britain are different from his reasons for starting the Blitz — make sure you understand exactly what each of them was intended to do. That's the key bit.

Safeguarding Britain's Food Supplies

Britain needed a strong <u>food supply</u> from abroad to <u>survive</u> during the war, just as in the First World War. Hitler realised this, and <u>U-boats</u> were used to <u>attack</u> British food supply ships in the Atlantic.

German U-boats attacked British food supplies

1) One of Germany's strategies was to <u>cut off</u> Britain's food supplies to <u>force</u> a peace settlement.
2) <u>U-boats</u> (submarines) were used to <u>sink ships</u> bringing food into British ports.
3) <u>Food supplies</u> began to run short in Britain from the beginning of the war.

Food rationing started in January 1940

1) <u>Rationing</u> was brought in in <u>January 1940</u> to make sure none of the really crucial stuff ran out.
2) The new <u>Ministry of Food</u> gave everyone a <u>ration book</u>.
3) <u>Stamps</u> in the book showed <u>how much</u> of each food a person was entitled to.
4) Rationing was brought in in <u>stages</u>.

Early 1940 — butter, bacon, sugar

Late 1940 — meat, TEA

1941 — jam

1942 — sweets

5) The Ministry of Food published healthy <u>recipes</u> which used non-rationed foods. They were especially keen on people eating lots of <u>vegetables</u> and <u>brown bread</u>.
6) <u>Pregnant women</u>, <u>babies</u> and <u>breastfeeding women</u> were given special rations.
7) Some foods that weren't rationed were in short supply too — stuff like <u>rice</u>, <u>peas</u>, <u>tomatoes</u>, <u>cereals</u>, and almost anything made with sugar like <u>syrup</u> and <u>treacle</u>. There was a '<u>black market</u>' in these.
8) There were <u>shortages</u> of lots of other stuff — <u>petrol</u>, <u>clothes</u>, <u>make up</u>, <u>crockery</u>, and <u>razor blades</u>.
9) A lot of people <u>grew their own</u> vegetables in allotments — "digging for victory".
10) Most people <u>didn't like rationing</u>, but they put up with it because they thought the <u>system</u> was fair.

By 1943 the U-boats were less of a threat

1) The worst year for the food supply ships was <u>1942</u>.
2) The Navy began a <u>convoy system</u> to protect ships.
3) Techniques for <u>finding</u> and <u>attacking</u> submarines got better — have a look at the picture for some of them.
4) Britain got faster at <u>building</u> new ships.
5) As the <u>U-boat threat diminished</u>, so did the <u>supply problem</u>. But <u>prices</u> went up an enormous <u>50%</u> between <u>1939-41</u> — talk about inflation!
6) Britain started to <u>grow more food</u> — less had to be imported.
7) The fight against the U-boats is called the <u>Battle of the Atlantic</u>.

Long-range bombers.

Radar & ASDIC — a kind of underwater radar system.

More powerful depth charges — underwater bombs.

The Ministry of Food — preaching healthy recipes...

This is another page of '<u>whys</u>'. Scribble down as many reasons as you can for <u>why</u> the U-boats attacked food supplies, <u>why</u> rationing started, and <u>why</u> U-boats were <u>less</u> of a problem by <u>1943</u>.

Conscription & The Role of Women

It's pretty obvious how being <u>called up</u> would change a man's life — he would have to leave home, learn how to fight and probably be sent abroad. But many women got called up too in this war. They didn't tend to get <u>sent abroad</u>, but there were still some <u>big changes</u> to their lives.

Men and women got called up

Men aged <u>18–41</u> were called up to fight — <u>unless</u> they worked in vital industries like <u>coal mining</u>, <u>steel working</u>, or building <u>ships</u>, <u>planes</u> or <u>weapons</u>.

From <u>1941</u> women could be called up if they were <u>single</u> and aged <u>20–30</u>. They could be asked to join the <u>Armed Services</u>, work on farms with the <u>Land Army</u> or work in <u>factories</u>. They weren't actually allowed to <u>fight</u> in the Army, and mostly stayed in Britain.

There were about <u>450 000</u> women in the Armed Services, and about <u>4 500 000</u> men.

Loads of the people who <u>weren't</u> called up <u>volunteered</u> for war work. They worked as <u>ambulance drivers</u>, <u>nurses</u>, <u>firemen</u> and <u>air wardens</u>.

The <u>Home Guard</u> was a <u>volunteer defence army</u> for men in reserved occupations, or too old or too unfit to join the Army. They didn't even have proper weapons to start with.

<u>Conscientious objectors</u> didn't have to fight.

Call for 100,000 women to do war work

COME INTO THE FACTORIES

Millions more women went to work

In <u>1931</u> there were about <u>5 000 000</u> women in work. By <u>1941</u> there were more like <u>14 000 000</u> women at work, either in the <u>Armed Services</u>, the <u>Land Army</u>, doing war-related jobs in the <u>factories</u>, or just doing <u>normal jobs</u>.

In almost all the jobs women only got a <u>fraction</u> of the pay men would have got for the <u>same work</u>.

Like everyone else they had to work <u>long hours</u> — <u>50-hour weeks</u> were quite normal.

FACTORY WORK

1) *7 000 000 women went to work, welding, making planes, guns and bombs, and sewing uniforms, barrage balloons, tents, and parachutes — all stuff that was vitally important to fighting the war.*

2) *Women often had to put up with a negative attitude from employers and co-workers.*

3) *Many women worked part-time so they could still run the house, do the shopping, look after the kids...*

THE WOMEN'S VOLUNTARY SERVICE

1) *1 million women joined the Women's Voluntary Service.*

2) *They did a lot of work clearing up after bombing raids, and recruiting women volunteers for other war work.*

3) *Slightly bizarre, but they also darned soldiers' socks and made 1 million pies a week for farm workers.*

THE LAND ARMY

1) *80 000 women joined the Women's Land Army.*

2) *The "Land Girls" went out to work on farms as part of the Government's drive to get more food grown in Britain, freeing up ships for transporting soldiers and arms.*

After the war some women had to <u>give up</u> their jobs — some were happy about it, but others missed their sense of <u>independence</u> and freedom.

Women were called up — no, not dodgy phone-calls...

Most of this page is about how <u>women</u> got involved in the war, but <u>don't forget</u> those 4 500 000 men in the forces. You need to know about the <u>kind of jobs</u> women did to help the war effort.

Censorship & Propaganda

The Government kept <u>strict tabs</u> on what information was getting through to <u>civilians</u> and people in the <u>Armed Forces</u>. Was it <u>thought control</u> or <u>sensible security</u>, I wonder.

The <u>Ministry of Information</u> controlled the news

CARELESS TALK COSTS LIVES

The Ministry of Information produced <u>films</u>, <u>radio broadcasts</u>, <u>leaflets</u> and <u>posters</u> telling a positive story, and encouraging a positive attitude.

The need is GROWING

DIG FOR VICTORY

The Ministry of Information was also in charge of giving people in Britain the official <u>news on the war</u>. They tended to <u>ignore failures</u> and <u>report success</u>.

The Government tried to <u>cover up</u> how many people were being <u>killed</u> by bombers in the Blitz (see P.39). News reports with pictures of the <u>dead</u> or <u>casualty figures</u> were censored. Most reports were <u>jolly</u> and <u>encouraging</u> — they concentrated on how <u>bravely</u> people were coping with the bombs, and the <u>numbers of enemy planes</u> that were shot down.

The story of Dunkirk told <u>at the time</u> was that hundreds of <u>brave men</u> in <u>plucky little boats</u> had <u>gallantly saved</u> the British and French soldiers. But most of the soldiers were evacuated by the <u>Royal Navy</u> — and the <u>bloody and chaotic struggle</u> to get to the boats was played down. The months after Dunkirk were particularly <u>tough</u> in Britain and the Government didn't want to lower people's <u>morale</u>.

Entertainment <u>let people</u> forget <u>about the war</u>

1) Entertainment <u>wasn't</u> going to win the war, but people needed <u>something</u> to give them a <u>break</u> from the grimness of life. The most popular entertainments were going to <u>cinemas</u> and <u>dance halls</u>.

2) There was entertainment for people in the <u>Army, Navy and Air Force</u>. <u>Stars</u> went out to perform for them. One of the most famous was a singer called <u>Vera Lynn</u> — the "Forces' sweetheart".

3) There was a special entertainment show on the British <u>radio</u> run by ENSA, the <u>Entertainments National Service Association</u>, also known as "Every Night Something Awful".

Churchill <u>wanted people to feel they were "all in it together"</u>

<u>Winston Churchill</u> became Prime Minister in <u>1940</u>. He was a <u>forceful</u> personality and people found it easy to <u>believe in</u> him. He was brilliant at <u>writing</u> and <u>delivering heroic speeches</u>, which were broadcast on the BBC to stir up people's <u>enthusiasm</u> and <u>determination</u> to win the war.

Two of Churchill's most important ideas were that British people were "all in it together", and that this was a "total war".

"<u>Total war</u>" meant every person in the country was playing an active part in the war. It wasn't all down to the government and the armed forces. Putting up with rationing or blackouts was a way for everyone to help.

The feeling that everyone was "<u>in it together</u>" had a powerful effect on the traditional class structure as <u>everybody</u> felt that they were making a valuable <u>contribution</u> to the war effort.

The <u>propaganda machine</u> — have a good look...

The <u>Blitz</u> and <u>Dunkirk</u> are brilliant examples of how the Government <u>controlled information</u> to make terrible events into something to be <u>proud</u> of. You'll need to understand "<u>total war</u>" as well.

D-Day & the Defeat of Germany

By 1942 things were changing. The USSR and USA had entered the war in 1941. It took another 3 years for Germany to be completely defeated though. The important stuff to learn on this page is what happened on D-Day, and what changed in Britain because of the war.

1942 was the turning point of the war

The entry of the USA into the war played a major part in turning the tide. But so did these three victories:

1) At El Alamein in North Africa, the British General Montgomery's "Desert Rats" defeated the German and Italian forces led by Rommel. Soon the enemy was pushed out of North Africa entirely.
2) By 1942 the Allies were winning the Battle of the Atlantic. More supplies could now get through.
3) The Soviet Army fought a large German army at Stalingrad. In February 1943 the Germans surrendered.

The invasion of Europe was launched on D-Day

1) In 1943 American and British forces invaded Italy. The Italians surrendered. This was the end of their alliance with Germany. The German army had to retreat Northwards, but continued to fight.
2) By spring 1944 the Allies were ready to try getting Germany out of France.
3) Portable harbours called 'mulberries' were prepared for landing tanks and heavy guns. A fuel pipeline was laid across the Channel.

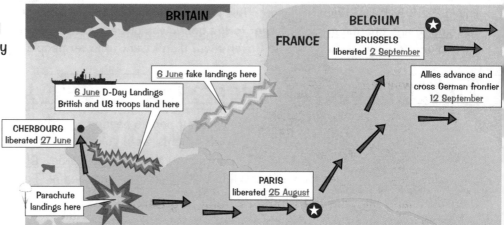

4) On 6th June 1944 the D-day landings began on beaches in Normandy. 326 000 soldiers were landed in the first week.
5) By 12th September the Army had reached the German frontier.
6) The Germans counter-attacked in December at the Battle of the Bulge. The Allies were pushed back a few miles through Belgium but only temporarily. This was Hitler's final gamble, but he refused to make peace.
7) The Allies kept on advancing towards Berlin. In the meantime the Soviet army was approaching from the East. In April 1945 the Russians captured Berlin, and the Germans surrendered on 7th May. The war in Europe was over.

What the end of the war meant for Britain...

1) Britain was in massive financial trouble. They owed their allies the USA millions of pounds. British industry was out of date. Overseas markets had been lost. It would take a long time for the British economy to recover. Rationing continued until 1954.
2) A new Labour government was elected in 1945. They began to set up the Welfare State. A lot of historians believe it was the bonding experience of the war that made this possible. Other people argue that these changes were coming anyway, and the war just delayed them.
3) About 600 000 people from Britain and the Commonwealth were killed in the war. But it could have been much worse if Britain had been invaded.

Who won the war — was it really Britain...

Learn the events of D-Day, and how the Allies followed it up with the push into Germany. Don't skip the bit about the effects of the war on Britain either. It's all important stuff.

Revision Summary

There's no point in pussyfooting around. If you want to get decent marks for the Second World War you're going to have to learn everything in this section. Doing these revision summary questions is a really good start. Try answering them all. Scribble your answers down, so you can check back in the section and see if you were right. If you got any wrong you need to learn those facts again. When you can answer all the questions on this page without even thinking, then you really know your stuff.

1) When did Britain declare war on Germany? Give the exact date.

2) List 5 things that were done to prepare for the air raids.

3) Why were Germans, Austrians and Italians put in internment camps?

4) Why was the part of the war up until spring 1940 called the "Phoney" War?

5) Who became British Prime Minister after Neville Chamberlain?

6) When did France surrender to Hitler?

7) What was Operation Sealion?
   a) a trip to Paignton b) a conservation project c) Hitler's plan to invade Britain?

8) List three advantages the RAF had over the Luftwaffe.

9) When did Hitler call off the Blitz? What did he want to do instead?

10) What's a U-boat?

11) When was jam rationed?

12) Give three reasons why U-boat attacks were less of a threat in 1943 than they were in 1940.

13) If you were a 40 year old man in 1941, working in a newsagents, was there a chance you might be called up?

14) How many men were there (roughly) in the Armed Services?

15) How many pies did the Women's Voluntary Services make each week?

16) What was the name of the Government department in charge of spreading news and propaganda about the war?

17) What did ENSA stand for (officially)?

18) What did Churchill mean by "total war"?

19) Name the 3 really important battles in 1942, that changed everything.

20) What's a 'mulberry'?

21) How many soldiers were landed on the beaches in the first week of the Normandy landings?

22) When was Berlin captured?

23) What kind of Government was elected just after the war?

Bake For Victory!

Planning for the Future

There's a big link between the "all in this together chaps" attitude in the Second World War, and the moves towards a welfare state — that's what quite a few historians reckon anyway.

The War changed attitudes to welfare

The Liberal Government of 1906–15 gave a lot of Government help to poor people (see *Section One*). At the time many people in the Conservative party and some Liberals thought it was wrong for the Government to be so involved in people's lives. The debate between people who supported Government involvement and those who didn't never died out. After the Second World War there was a big swing in favour of giving more help.

1) Thousands of millions of pounds were spent on fighting the war. The attitude to spending changed — people felt if a Government could deal with the worst poverty by spending lots of money then that's what they should do.

2) In order to win the war, the National Government took control of health and social services, through policies like rationing food. They had to make sure people ate a healthy diet — and as a result health improved. Many people felt if the Government could do this in wartime, they should carry on in peacetime.

3) There were lots of Labour party politicians in the National government during the war. They felt strongly about the suffering of the "hungry thirties" and wanted to make sure that Britain had seen the last of that kind of poverty.

4) Housing was already a problem before the Second World War. During the war, huge numbers of houses were bombed — and huge numbers of people were made homeless. The problem was now very bad — it'd need some kind of drastic solution after the war.

5) Lots of middle-class people only realised how bad life was for poor people from the cities when they hosted evacuee kids. The children were dirty, their clothes were falling to bits, and they seemed underfed. Lots of them had never even had a bed of their own.

The Beveridge Report — "From the cradle to the grave"

During the Second World War the Government set up a committee to look into British welfare and suggest how to improve it. William Beveridge, who had worked on some of the Liberal reforms of 1906–1914 (see P.1-P.6) wrote the final report, which was published in November 1942. Officially called "Social Insurance and Allied Services" it's more usually known as The Beveridge Report.

1) The Beveridge Report sold 635 000 copies. That's a massive amount for a dry, serious government report. It captured the public imagination.

2) Beveridge referred to the big problems facing poor people as the 'Five Giants': Want, Disease, Ignorance, Squalor and Idleness.

3) The Report said the Government should introduce more insurance schemes, more housing, child allowances, a national health service and a policy of full employment and secondary education for all. This would protect people from the Five Giants "from the cradle to the grave".

4) Beveridge thought the scheme should replace all others. It should be universal — for everybody, not just the poorest people.

5) He suggested everyone pay weekly contributions to a government-run insurance scheme — which would pay them benefit if they were out of work, sick or disabled. There would be no more means testing.

GO BEVERIDGE!

LABOUR

Oh, no, no, no, no, no, no, no Beveridge. Not till after the war.

CONSERVATIVES

Labour MPs were generally for the Beveridge Report and wanted to see it put into practice straightaway. Conservative MPs including Churchill wanted to wait until after the war — and didn't seem so enthusiastic.

The Beveridge Report — I'll drink to that...

Things were changing. Look at how the war affected attitudes to welfare. Make sure you know what the Beveridge Report was about — what the five giants were and how they could be tackled.

Creating the Welfare State

A report isn't the same thing as actually sorting out the problems. It took time to get things done.

Two Giants were tackled under Churchill...

Beveridge's Five Giants were Ignorance, Idleness, Want, Disease and Squalor.
The National Government began the fight against the first two during the last years of the War.

It's odd to think the MPs in Westminster were debating the age of school leavers while war was raging on the Continent and all around the world.

Ignorance — The Education Act

1) The Education Act was passed in 1944.

2) The politician behind the Education Act was R.A. Butler, President of the Board of Education. The Education Act is sometimes called the Butler Act.

3) Fees for state secondary schools were abolished, so everybody could afford to go. Primary schools were already free.

4) The school leaving age was raised from 14 to 15, starting from 1947. It was put up to 16 in 1973.

5) The Act said state primary and secondary schools would be run by Local Education Authorities (LEAs).

6) Everyone in their last year at primary school had to take a test called the 11+ to see what kind of secondary school they'd go to. Grammar schools were for the most academic kids. Technical schools were for those with good practical skills. Secondary moderns took everyone else.

Idleness — the aim was 'full employment'

Beveridge (again) wrote a *White Paper* on Employment Policy published in 1944. The Paper said that all governments should try to get full employment. 3% unemployment should be the absolute maximum.

White Paper = statement of what the government hopes/plans to do

Unemployment did actually stay below 3% for about 20 years after the end of the war.

Labour won the General Election in 1945

At the end of the War in Europe, the Labour Party left the National Government and an election was called.

1) Voters only really trusted the Labour Party to put the Beveridge Report into practice.

2) Soldiers were particularly keen on a better life after the war, and lots of them voted Labour.

3) Despite Churchill's leadership during the war, many people remembered the Conservatives' failures during the 1930s. Churchill said Britain was too poor to set up a welfare state yet.

4) Labour won the General Election in 1945 with a massive majority of seats.

5) The new Prime Minister was Clement Attlee, who had been Deputy PM during the war.

Creating the Welfare State

The Labour Government set up the Welfare State...

Want — The National Insurance Act

1) The National Insurance Act was passed in 1946. It extended Lloyd George's scheme from 1911 (P.4) to cover all working adults. Everyone in work paid a small amount of national insurance every week. Employers added a contribution, recorded on the employee's insurance cards. Everyone who had paid into the scheme could claim benefits when they were ill, unemployed, or retired (at 60 for women, 65 for men).

The act also allowed for pensions for widows, funeral grants and maternity grants to be paid out of the National Insurance money.

2) The National Insurance (Industrial Injuries) Act was passed in 1946 too. It paid special benefits to people injured at work, including disability benefit.

3) The National Assistance Act passed in 1948 set up the National Assistance Board. This helped people on really low incomes. The Public Assistance Committees that used to do this were scrapped. Even though National Assistance was only meant to be for the worst cases more and more people applied. It was later called Supplementary Benefit.

4) Back in 1945, the National Government passed the Children's Allowances Act. All children after the first one got 5 shillings a week.

Disease — The National Health Service

1) The National Health Service gave free medical, dental, optical and hospital care to everyone.

2) The laws setting up the National Health Service were passed in 1946. The service began in 1948.

3) Almost all of Britain's hospitals were now in the Health Service, and run by 14 regional hospital boards.

4) Maternity care , health visitors and child welfare clinics were set up too, and run by local authorities.

5) The man in charge of these reforms was the Minister of Health, Aneurin Bevan.

6) The idea could have been scuppered before it got off the ground. Doctors, dentists and opticians used to charge their patients. Bevan first wanted them to be paid a salary — making them employees of the state. The British Medical Association kicked up a fuss about this. Bevan persuaded them to support the NHS by keeping doctors self-employed, but paying them a fee based on the number of patients they had.

7) Totally free treatment for everyone didn't last long — charges for glasses and false teeth were brought in in 1951, followed by prescription charges in 1952.

8) Overall the NHS massively improved the health of British people.

Squalor — new towns and new housing

There were two acts designed to ease the housing shortage.

The New Towns Act, 1946	The Town and Country Planning Act, 1947
Whole new towns could be planned and built by development corporations. The earliest ones were around London, designed to soak up some of the overflow: Stevenage, Harlow, and Welwyn Garden City.	*The act introduced the idea of carefully planning towns and villages in advance. All local authorities were expected to come up with a 20-year plan for land use. This led to far more council estates being built to provide cheap housing.*

Britain menaced by five giants? — you're having me on...

The stuff on this page is really worth learning. Yup, I know it's a lot of boring Acts — but it's the sort of thing you can't do history without: FACTS. Scribble down the NHS stuff and learn it too.

Nationalisation

The Welfare State was only part of the Labour Government's policy. They also brought in nationalisation. This economics stuff isn't easy, so don't feel gloomy if you don't get it first time.

Nationalisation is when the Government runs industry

In the 1930s, during the Depression (see *Section Five — The Depression*) people began to think that really serious unemployment and hardship could be reduced or even avoided if the Government planned the economy instead of leaving it to run itself.

Nationalisation was an important part of a planned economy. The Government would control the "means of production, distribution and exchange" — industry, transport and trade. This would allow them to make businesses more efficient, improve conditions for the workers, and invest money in big projects like road or house building to create new jobs for the unemployed.

The Labour Government nationalised some industries

After the Second World War the British economy was in poor shape.

1) Its industries were out-dated and inefficient, and Britain's export trade had practically disappeared.

2) Britain owed over £3000 million in loans — mostly to the USA.

The new Labour Government needed to modernise industry quickly in order to rebuild trade, and to create jobs for the soldiers returning from the war. They decided to nationalise some industries. If the Government owned them, the profits would go to the Government — and would help to pay for the Welfare State.

The first step was taken in 1946.

* The Bank of England was taken over by the Government. The Government could now make money available whenever they wanted to invest in industry.

The second step was to nationalise some of the biggest industries.

* Labour hoped that combining all the little mines, or power stations or bus companies into one national company would make them more efficient and even out prices and quality of service around the country.

* Each industry was run by a board of experts. The National Coal Board organised the coal industry. The British Transport Commission looked at ways of coordinating bus, train and boat services.

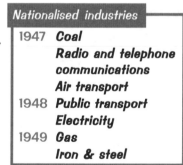

Nationalised industries	
1947	**Coal**
	Radio and telephone communications
	Air transport
1948	**Public transport**
	Electricity
1949	**Gas**
	Iron & steel

Labour's policies — successes or failures...

1) By 1950, Britain was recovering from the Second World War: exports were increasing, and there was full employment. The Welfare State had improved the standard of living for many people.

2) But rationing was still in place, and there was a housing shortage. Britain had also been drawn into the Korean War in 1950. In the 1951 General Election the Conservatives won and came back into power.

3) Nationalisation of inefficient and out-dated industries had been supported by all parties — but the Conservatives felt that Iron and Steel were profitable industries, and de-nationalised them in 1953.

4) Labour had created a "mixed economy" with some nationalisation — but not enough for many socialists.

5) Labour didn't have real expert economic planners — they had no overall plan, and just dealt with specific problems when they came up. The Welfare State was expensive, and may have held the economy back.

Cheap gin and tonic — my kind of mixed economy...

Nobody's expecting you to go on Newsnight and explain the pros and cons of a planned economy. The things to learn are why Labour tried nationalisation and which industries got nationalised.

Revision Summary

The Welfare State is one of those topics you've got to know inside out — why it happened, what it actually was, and how well it worked. If that sounds like a tall order, then that's what these questions are for — making sure you know the facts. Work your way through them — then, if there's anything you haven't got clear in your mind, go back through the section and learn it. After that, yep, you've guessed it — have another go at the questions. You should be able to sail through the whole lot.

1) After the Second World War was the general mood in favour of welfare or against it?

2) What made lots of middle-class people realise how bad life was for poor people living in cities?

3) What was the name of the famous report about welfare improvements published in 1942?

4) What were the 'five giants' referred to in the report?

5) Who was most enthusiastic about the report — Labour politicians or Conservatives?

6) What was the school leaving age set by the Butler Education Act (1944)?

7) Who did the Education Act say should run state primary and secondary schools?

   a) LEAs b) ELAs c) EELs

8) What percentage of unemployment did Beveridge say should be the absolute maximum?

9) How many people were out of work in the 20 years after the war?

10) Who won the 1945 General Election — Labour or the Conservatives?

11) Who was the new Prime Minister?

12) How did the National Insurance Act (1946) work?

   a) Everyone paid a small amount each week, and employers added a contribution. All those who paid into the scheme could claim benefits when they were ill, unemployed or retired.

   b) Everyone put half of their wages into a fund each week, and it was sent to the Government who used it to insure the nation against another war.

13) When the National Health Service started all treatments were free. What two types of treatment did people have to start paying for in 1951?

14) What did people have to start paying for in 1952?

15) How many regional hospital boards were there?

16) What year was the Town and Country Planning Act passed?

17) Name 2 new towns built in the 1940s.

18) What is nationalisation?

19) Give two reasons why Labour nationalised some industries after the Second World War.

20) Name two industries Labour nationalised between 1947 and 1949.

21) Give two reasons why Labour's policies could be seen as successes..

22) Give two reasons why Labour's policies could be seen as failures.

WELFARE STATE

Ireland in 1916

The topic of Ireland is a nightmare — you've absolutely <u>got</u> to get the background <u>clear</u> or you'll be <u>lost</u> later on. It's a topic people have <u>strong opinions</u> about — getting the <u>facts</u> is crucial.

Problems in Ireland go back a long time

1) The English began the <u>conquest</u> of Ireland in the <u>Middle Ages</u>. At many different times the Irish <u>fought back</u>.

2) When England became Protestant in <u>1534</u>, the Irish stayed loyal to the <u>Catholic church</u>.

3) After <u>1590</u>, the English Government encouraged <u>Scottish and English Protestants</u> to <u>settle</u> in Ireland.

4) In <u>1649</u>, England's Puritan (Protestant) leader Oliver Cromwell <u>crushed</u> an Irish rebellion.

5) In <u>1690</u>, an Irish army supporting the *deposed* Catholic King of England, James II, was <u>defeated</u> by the <u>new</u> Protestant English King, William of Orange, at the <u>Battle of the Boyne</u>.

deposed = made to give up the throne

6) Since <u>1800</u>, the Irish had <u>not</u> been allowed <u>their own parliament</u>. They were ruled from London.

> In <u>1845</u> and <u>'46</u>, the potato crop <u>failed</u>. It was the <u>main food source</u> in Ireland.
> Thousands <u>died</u> of starvation. Millions emigrated to Australia and North America.
> The population dropped from <u>8 million</u> in <u>1841</u> to just over <u>4 million</u> by <u>1914</u>.

Irish Nationalists wanted Home Rule for Ireland

By the beginning of the <u>twentieth century</u>, the population of Ireland was roughly split into two main groups.

1) Protestant <u>Unionists</u> mainly lived in the North. They wanted Ireland to be <u>part of the United Kingdom</u>.

2) Most <u>Nationalists</u> were Catholics from the South of Ireland. They wanted:

> 1) <u>Home Rule</u>: Ireland to have its own parliament, but still remain loyal to the British King.
>
> 2) <u>Land reform</u>: English landlords to give up their land. Land to be fairly shared out between the tenant farmers.

3) Several attempts were made during the nineteenth century to get the British Parliament to <u>vote</u> for Irish Home Rule — but each attempt <u>failed</u>. Then in <u>1912</u> a <u>new Home Rule Bill</u> was introduced.

4) The Unionist Protestants <u>hated</u> the idea, but the Catholics in the South were <u>all for it</u>. Both sides <u>raised armies</u>. In <u>1912</u> the Unionist Protestants recruited 100 000 people. The Nationalists formed an army of 75 000 'Irish Volunteers' in <u>1913</u>. There was <u>violence</u> on both sides.

The Easter Rising 1916

The Home Rule Bill was passed in <u>1914</u>, but <u>suspended</u> while Britain fought the First World War. Many Irishmen <u>volunteered</u> for the British Army — but some Nationalists felt it was time to <u>break completely</u> from Britain.

On Easter Monday, <u>24 April 1916</u>, an armed group led by <u>Patrick Pearse</u> occupied several official buildings in Dublin, including the <u>Law Courts</u> and the <u>General Post Office</u>. They flew a <u>green flag</u> over these buildings, and declared an Irish Republic <u>free</u> of British rule.

<u>Hardly anyone</u> in Dublin supported the rising. After 5 days, the British army won back control by firing on the rebels until they <u>gave up</u>. A rebel plot to get <u>help</u> from the <u>Germans</u> was discovered — and Pearse and fifteen other rebel leaders were <u>shot</u> by firing squads. Even people who <u>hadn't</u> supported the rising were <u>shocked</u> at the shootings. It made them feel more <u>sympathetic</u> towards the Nationalists.

Phew — this is really complicated stuff...

It's really important to understand who the <u>two main groups</u> of people in Ireland were, <u>and</u> what they wanted for Ireland. You've got to know all about <u>Home Rule</u> and the <u>Easter Rising</u> (<u>1916</u>) too.

Divided Ireland

The executions at the end of the Easter Rising changed the mood in Ireland. Many Nationalists stopped volunteering for the war, angering the Unionists. The rebels of 1916 became heroes.

Sinn Fein wanted independence for Ireland

1) The surviving rebels from 1916 went to prison. On their release, they and many others joined the Sinn Fein party — which said Ireland should be a free Republic.

2) In 1918, there was a British General Election. The older Nationalist Party won a few seats, but Sinn Fein won a big majority of the seats set aside for Irish MPs in Westminster — 73 out of 105.

3) The Sinn Fein MPs refused to go to Westminster, and set up a new parliament in Dublin called the Dail, with a government, police force, and law courts. It was led by a survivor from 1916 called Eamon de Valera.

4) Another survivor, Michael Collins, organised volunteer soldiers into the Irish Republican Army.

War broke out between the UK and the IRA in 1919

1) The British arrested Republican leaders and banned all talk of independence. But Collins escaped and began a guerrilla war against the British — organising murder squads, bombings and spying. The Anglo-Irish War lasted from 1919-1921.

2) The British Government formed a special force of ex-soldiers called the 'Black and Tans' to support the police in Ireland and end the IRA's violence. They were brutal in their methods.

3) Both sides committed terrible atrocities. On 21 November 1920, IRA men murdered 14 British agents in their homes or hotels. Later that day, the Black and Tans fired into a crowd of 8000 at a Gaelic football match, killing 12 people and wounding 70. But this reaction only drove more Irish people to support the IRA.

The Catholic South became a separate country

By late 1920, both sides were sick of the war. The British offered Home Rule, but the Unionists in the North were afraid that an Irish parliament would have more Republican MPs, and would choose independence. Therefore, in the Government of Ireland Act (1920), the British decided to split Ireland into two parts, the North and the South. Michael Collins accepted this in the Anglo-Irish treaty (1921), though he knew many in Sinn Fein would not accept the partition.

The Anglo-Irish Treaty (1921)

1) The 26 southern counties of Ireland became a separate country, with its own government.

2) The new Free State wasn't completely free of Britain though — it was still part of the Empire.

3) The other 6 counties in the North of Ireland would still be part of the UK, but with their own parliament in Belfast.

De Valera refused to accept the treaty — Sinn Fein split and there was a bloody civil war. Collins became leader of the Irish Free State, but was killed in 1922. The civil war ended soon after.

1937	Under the leadership of Eamon de Valera a new constitution was introduced. The country was renamed Eire.
1939-45	Eire refused to join in the Second World War, and declared it was a neutral country. Britain was unable to use the ports for Naval bases, and this added to problems in the North Atlantic. Eire did help Northern Ireland with the worst effects of bombing raids though.
1949	Prime Minister John Costello took Eire out of the Commonwealth. It was now the Republic of Ireland with no link to the British monarchy.
1955	Eire got international recognition when it joined the United Nations. Eire refused to join NATO, because they couldn't be allies with Britain, the 'occupying force' in the North.

The Troubles 1967–1972

In the late <u>1960s</u> and early <u>1970s</u>, relations between <u>Irish Republicans</u> and the <u>British</u> were especially <u>strained</u> and <u>violent</u>. Don't get caught up with whose fault it was — just learn the <u>facts</u>.

Catholics in Northern Ireland felt mistreated

After the treaty of <u>1921</u>, Northern Ireland had <u>stayed united</u> with Britain. Protestant Unionists <u>dominated</u> politics and appeared to have <u>better jobs</u> and <u>homes</u>. Many Catholics in the North felt like <u>second-class citizens</u>. This made them even more keen on a <u>united free Ireland</u>.

> ### Problems for Catholics in Northern Ireland:
> - It was <u>hard</u> to get on the <u>electoral roll</u> — which means it was <u>hard</u> to <u>get a vote</u>.
> - Constituency <u>boundaries</u> were <u>fixed</u> to give Unionist candidates the <u>best chance</u> of election success.
> - The <u>health services</u> and <u>transport</u> in Catholic areas were <u>worse</u> than in Protestant areas.
> - It was hard to get a <u>council house</u>, or decent <u>jobs</u> or <u>education</u>.
> - <u>Violent</u> and <u>unfair treatment</u> from the Police — the Royal Ulster Constabulary (RUC), and the 'B Specials'.

Catholic protests led to minor reforms

Protestant Unionists

Orangemen = Committed Unionists. Named after William of Orange (see P.49)

1967	Catholics and sympathisers formed a <u>Civil Rights Movement</u> to organise protests and marches to complain about their treatment.
October 1968	Civil Rights march to Londonderry. Protestant *Orangemen* were outraged — the march was <u>broken up</u> by the RUC.
1969	The Provisional IRA <u>split</u> from the official IRA. The 'Provos' were committed to <u>military action</u> to <u>drive out</u> the British.
August 1969	<u>Fighting</u> between Catholics and Protestants got <u>out of control</u>. The Northern Irish government asked for British help — and the <u>army</u> was sent in to safeguard the rights of <u>all citizens</u>, not just Protestants. <u>Reform</u> was needed fast.

British Home Secretary <u>James Callaghan</u> began a series of reforms to try to reassure the Catholic community.

- 'B' specials abolished.
- RUC reorganised and disarmed
- Fairer system for allocating council houses.
- Fairer electoral district system.

But the fighting didn't stop

The Provisional IRA began a <u>terrorist campaign</u> and the troops had to start searching Catholic houses for weapons and suspects — and <u>clashes</u> broke out.

Internment = <u>suspected terrorists</u> can be held in prison <u>without</u> having a trial

February 1971	An IRA gunman killed a British soldier — the first to die in the Troubles.
August 1971	The Stormont Government introduced *internment*. Fighting got worse.
early 1972	Provisionals were soon <u>controlling</u> Catholic streets — these became '<u>no-go</u>' areas for the police and army. IRA and Provisional soldiers openly walk the streets of Belfast and Londonderry. The Protestants had soldiers too: the <u>Ulster Volunteer Force</u> and the <u>Ulster Defence Association</u>.
January 1972	<u>30 January</u> was "<u>Bloody Sunday</u>" — British troops clashed with a Catholic Civil Rights march in Londonderry, and <u>fired</u> on the crowd, <u>killing</u> 13 people and wounding many others.
March 1972	Violence on all sides was <u>out of control</u>. World opinion <u>condemned</u> the British policy. The Stormont Government was <u>abolished</u> and '<u>Direct Rule</u>' was introduced to try to <u>stop</u> a civil war.

Get these dates learnt — they're seriously important...

Learn the <u>problems</u> Catholics faced in Northern Ireland — and <u>all</u> those dates. It might not look like a lot of fun to learn, but it's really important to get the <u>order of events</u> clear now.

Obstacles to Peace

In the 1970s and 1980s there were continual efforts to find a peaceful settlement for Northern Ireland. Trouble was there were some problems that stood in the way, and they weren't easy to fix.

Protestants and Catholics wouldn't work together

> In Northern Ireland people have always tended to vote for somebody because he or she is a Catholic Nationalist, or Protestant Unionist. During the last 30 years, there have been more Protestants than Catholics. That made it hard for Catholics to get elected. The idea behind power-sharing was to give the Catholics more say in the way Northern Ireland was run.

In 1974, the British Government tried to set up an Assembly and Executive to rule Northern Ireland, with a fairer share of power for Catholics.

Reserved for Catholic

- Members of the Assembly were elected, but Catholics had guaranteed seats on the Executive.
- But a lot of Protestants felt the Catholics got too many seats in the Executive — 4 out of 11.
- They held a General Strike, and brought life in Northern Ireland to a standstill.
- After five months of strikes the British Government dropped the power-sharing scheme.

In 1982, Margaret Thatcher's government had another go at setting up a new Irish Assembly. This time it was the Catholics who refused to join, and the attempt failed.

The Police and Army seemed to be against Catholics

> Most soldiers and police officers in Northern Ireland are Protestants.
> Many Catholics see the British army as an occupying force, who are mostly
> interested in looking after the Protestants, not in keeping the peace in general.

The Royal Ulster Constabulary is the Northern Irish police force. For a while it was controlled by the army, but in 1977 it was handed back into police control. Even today most officers are Protestants.

The Ulster Defence Regiment was the main army regiment operating in Northern Ireland during the 1970s and 1980s. The force was mainly Protestant, worked closely with the RUC, and was unpopular with Catholics. In 1993, the UDR became the Royal Irish Regiment. This new regiment was meant to be more Catholic-friendly.

Numbers of troops have been continually cut back — but their strategies got tougher and tougher:

1) Plastic bullets used to break up riots.
2) Informants planted in terrorist groups.
3) Undercover SAS missions.
4) Suspected IRA terrorists shot dead.

The IRA continued their campaign in and out of prison

IRA prisoners were kept at the Maze Prison, in high security 'H' blocks. They kept up protests from the prison — they wanted to embarrass the British Government, and keep Nationalist support.

1972	The British Government agreed to treat IRA prisoners as political prisoners. They no longer had to work in prison or wear prison uniform.
1976	These privileges were abolished. IRA prisoners began the "Blanket Protest", going round in nothing but blankets, so they wouldn't have to wear the uniform.
1978	IRA prisoners began smearing their own faeces on the walls of their cells — to annoy the guards and make a point about the conditions they lived in.
1980	IRA prisoners began hunger strikes at the Maze as a protest.
1981	Bobby Sands died of starvation — followed by 10 others that year.

The Last Twenty Years

British and Irish politicians, the people of Northern Ireland, and politicians from abroad have tried to find a solution to the problems. You need to learn what people have tried, what's worked, and what hasn't worked. There are no short cuts for learning it — only good hard graft.

In 1980 talks started with Eire about reuniting Ireland

1) After 1980, Margaret Thatcher's Government tried a new approach. They said they would let Northern Ireland join Eire if that's what the majority of people wanted.

2) In 1984, Eire suggested combining the Northern and Southern parts of Ireland without waiting for majority agreement. Margaret Thatcher refused to go this far, but talks continued.

3) The Anglo-Irish Agreement (sometimes called the Hillsborough Agreement) was signed by Britain and Ireland (Eire) in 1985. A joint committee of the two governments would discuss the big issues in Northern Ireland — the security forces, policing, the law and the judicial system.

Talks were held with the Nationalists in the 1990s

1) Senior British civil servants started holding secret talks with Sinn Fein in 1991.

2) In 1993 Bill Clinton (the President of the United States) urged Sinn Fein to cooperate, and invited their leader Gerry Adams to visit the USA. Sinn Fein was by now seen as the IRA's political wing.

3) The SDLP (another republican political party) and the IRA had their own talks. The IRA agreed they would consider a ceasefire if the British Government came up with a way of beginning talks.

4) The Downing Street Declaration was made in 1993. It was a joint statement by the British and Irish Prime Ministers, saying they wanted to encourage talks between all people in Ireland.

5) The IRA and the main Unionist terrorist groups called a ceasefire in 1994.

6) The British then began to demand that the Provisional IRA give up their weapons. The IRA felt they were being pushed too far, too fast. They broke the ceasefire in 1996, bombing Canary Wharf, and then Manchester city centre. Sinn Fein were now excluded from the peace talks.

The Labour Government began fresh talks in 1997

1) Labour won the May 1997 British General Election. Tony Blair wanted peace talks. The IRA declared a new ceasefire and talks began again between Britain, Eire, and political parties from Northern Ireland. The talks were chaired by US Senator George Mitchell.

2) The talks ended on 9 April 1998. On that day, it was announced that a new power-sharing assembly would be set up in Northern Ireland, and Eire would give up the idea of a united Ireland.

THIS WAS CALLED THE GOOD FRIDAY AGREEMENT

3) All the people of Ireland, North and South, voted on the Agreement in a referendum. 71% of people in the North were for it, and 94% in the South.

4) There were elections in June 1998 for the new Assembly, and Stormont reopened for business in July.

5) Part of the Good Friday Agreement said all sides should give up their weapons. This was called 'decommissioning'. The Canadian General, John de Chastelain, held talks with the different terrorist groups to work out how to do this in practice. He reported on 30 June 1999.

6) Unionists didn't believe that the IRA would give up their weapons. At first they refused to join talks on setting up an actual Government for Northern Ireland, but after long negotiations Direct Rule was handed over to Northern Ireland on 1 December 1999. The First Minister was the Unionist David Trimble.

7) Since then all sides have worked at finding a permanent peaceful settlement — but decommissioning has continued to be a major issue.

The answer to the Irish question — they're still looking...

There's a huge amount to learn on these two pages, I'm afraid. Drawing a timeline with dates and the main events is probably your best bet for learning the facts — I know it's dull, but it's worth it.

Revision Summary

The key to the topic of the UK and Ireland is knowing what happened when. The order things happened in is really important for trying to explain how one event led to another; eg how the Easter Rising led to a growth of support for Sinn Fein. And the best way to check you've got all the facts straight is by testing yourself now with these questions — and sticking at it until you've got the whole lot clear and correct.

1) When did the English first conquer Ireland?

2) What important event in Irish history happened in 1690?

3) Name the two main groups of people in Ireland in the twentieth century?

4) What did Home Rule mean?

5) What did the members of the Easter Rising of 1916 want for Ireland?

6) What happened to Patrick Pearse and fifteen other leaders of the Easter Rising?

7) What effect did this have?

   a) It stopped Germany helping the Irish b) It changed the mood in Ireland against the British

8) What did the Sinn Fein party want for Ireland?

9) What did the Sinn Fein MPs elected to Parliament in 1918 do instead of going to Westminster?

10) What was the name of the man who organised the IRA and started a guerrilla war?

   a) Eamon de Valera   b) Patrick Pearse   c) Gerry Adams   d) Michael Collins

11) What was the name of the British force of ex-soldiers who committed many atrocities?

12) What were the main points of the Peace Treaty of 1921?

13) Why was there a civil war in Ireland over the Treaty?

   a) because many in Sinn Fein refused to accept it   b) because de Valera hated Collins

14) What did Eire do during the Second World War (1939-1945)?

15) Give examples of two problems faced by Catholics in Northern Ireland after 1921.

16) What was the difference between the offical IRA and the Provisional IRA?

17) What was 'internment'?

18) What was 'Direct Rule'? When was it brought in by the British Government?

19) Give two major problems which are obstacles to peace in Northern Ireland?

20) What was the Anglo-Irish Agreement (1985)?

21) What was the Good Friday Agreement (1998)?

The Suez Crisis, 1956

This topic looks like an odd one to start with. There are huge chunks of time between the three wars in the section — the Suez, the Falklands and the Gulf. What it's really about is the way Britain's reputation as an international player has changed. And there are only three pages to learn.

The Suez Canal was Britain's short cut to India

1) The French government had originally built the Suez canal to join the Mediterranean Sea with the Red Sea. It opened in 1869.

2) Britain wanted fast and easy access to India for trade and defence, and bought shares in the Canal. Troops were stationed round the Canal. Egypt became a British colony. In the Second World War, German forces tried to capture the Canal, but Britain managed to hang on to it.

3) After the Second World War, Egypt got independence from Britain, and a British-friendly government was set up. In 1952 there was a revolution — Britain agreed to withdraw from the Canal Zone, but kept their shares in the Canal.

Egypt took control of the Canal in 1956

1) The new ruler of Egypt, Colonel Gamal Nasser, was keen on reforming and modernising Egypt. He wanted to build a huge dam across the Nile at Aswan for irrigation and generating electricity.

2) The USA offered to help pay for the dam. They then found out that Egypt was buying Russian-made tanks, planes and arms. The USA refused to deal with anyone who was dealing with Russia.

3) Nasser still needed to pay for the dam. The Suez Canal Company was a massively profitable business, and Nasser took it over in 1956 so he could use the profits to pay for the dam.

4) Britain and France were very cheesed off. They were worried that the oil supply from the Middle East would be cut off. Nasser said shareholders would get compensation, and that ships from all countries except Israel would be allowed to use the Canal, but this didn't convince Britain and France.

5) Sir Anthony Eden, the British Prime Minister, was keen to find a solution to the crisis. His Cabinet, the French government and MI6 wanted military action — they felt strong action should be taken immediately, instead of trying to appease Nasser the same way Hitler had been appeased in 1938.

Britain and France Got Egg on Their Faces

Britain, France and Israel made a secret pact. Israel would attack Egypt. When Egypt fought back, Britain and France would call for the fighting to stop. They didn't really want Egypt to back down — it was an excuse to send in troops. In October 1956 that's exactly what happened. Israel attacked and Egypt fought back. When the fighting didn't stop, Britain and France bombed Egypt's airbases and sent troops into the Canal Zone. Nasser closed down the Canal, and sank merchant ships.

BUT: the USSR and the USA both announced that they thought the attack on Egypt was completely unnecessary aggression. This was during the Cold War when the USSR and USA didn't agree about anything, so they must have felt very strongly. The United Nations called for immediate withdrawal.

Britain and France couldn't get oil while the Canal was closed. They also couldn't keep up their aggressive stance with the rest of the world against them. They agreed to a ceasefire on 6 November and began to withdraw troops. United Nations peacekeepers were sent in to police the Canal and the border between Egypt and Israel.

OVERALL RESULTS

1) Britain had tried to behave as though they were still running an Empire in the Middle East. Instead they were humiliated, and the USA withdrew support for the pound — which caused a fall in Britain's gold reserves.

2) Eden was exhausted by the crisis and resigned. His Chancellor Harold Macmillan became Prime Minister.

3) The USA had played a big part in getting Britain to pull out of Suez. This made Britain look weak at making decisions, and unable to manage international relations without US help. Britain was no longer a world power.

The Falklands War, 1982

At first sight, this seems like a lot of fuss over sheep and penguins — but it rebuilt British pride...

British people settled in the Falklands in 1833

1) The Falkland Islands are about 400 miles from Argentina in the South Atlantic. That's 8000 miles from Britain.
2) British sheep farmers settled in the Falklands in 1833, and stayed. In 1982 they still wanted to be British.
3) The Argentinians call the islands the Malvinas, and claim they actually belong to Argentina.
4) By 1982 negotiations about handing the islands over to Argentina had been going on for about 20 years, but had made no real progress. Argentina had the impression that Britain was losing interest in the Falklands, especially when an aircraft carrier stationed there was scrapped. The US Government also gave Argentina the impression that it would not get involved in any quarrel over the islands.

Argentina's invasion in 1982 was unexpected

1) General Galtieri, the military dictator who ruled Argentina, launched an attack in April 1982. Argentinian soldiers and marines occupied the capital, Port Stanley, and another island further out in the Atlantic, South Georgia. The British Governor was sent back to London.
2) The British Government in London hadn't been expecting this at all. The Foreign Secretary Lord Carrington resigned. The UN and EEC protested to Argentina, but they wouldn't budge.

Go on lads. Keep the Falklands British

Margaret Thatcher decided on war

1) Margaret Thatcher appealed to the UN to resolve the problem. At the same time a British Task Force of 79 ships and 6000 troops was put together. Ships included an aircraft carrier called *Hermes*, and troop carriers.
2) The Task Force set off for the Falklands while peace negotiations went on at the UN. The USA helped the British by allowing the Task Force to refuel on Ascension Island in the Atlantic. After 3 weeks, the Force arrived.
3) When the Task Force arrived in Falklands waters, they drew an imaginary line around the islands, and said any Argentine ships inside it would be sunk — it was called the Total Exclusion Zone. South Georgia was quickly recaptured, and an Argentinian cruiser called the *General Belgrano*, carrying troops and missiles, was sunk. 368 Argentinians died — it was very controversial because the ship was outside the Exclusion Zone.
4) British troops landed at San Carlos Bay on 21 May 1982, despite heavy bombardment of their ships beforehand. Helicopters were damaged in the fighting and soldiers had to get to Port Stanley on foot.
5) There were 15 000 Argentinian troops in the Falklands. Most of them were inexperienced new recruits. The British force was made up of well-trained professional soldiers. After British victories at Darwin and Goose Green, the Argentinians were encircled and Port Stanley was recaptured.
6) Argentina surrendered on 14 June 1982. Argentinian soldiers were shipped home.

OVERALL RESULTS

1) Britain kept the Falklands. This gave a clear message that Britain would defend her rights abroad.
2) Britain had acted alone and decisively, but with unofficial US support.
3) There was a huge surge of patriotic feeling in Britain. Margaret Thatcher became extremely popular, and the war helped the Conservatives win the 1983 General Election.
4) There were also critics of the war in Britain. 250 British soldiers and 750 Argentinians were killed. The financial cost to Britain was £1600 million, which seemed a lot of money for some islands.
5) The sinking of the Belgrano was remembered as an unprincipled act in Britain and abroad.
6) The Argentinian Government at the time was a military dictatorship. It was looking for a victory to distract people from problems at home. World opinion didn't fully support Britain, but it didn't support Argentina (unlike during Suez, when world opinion was opposed to Britain and France). Thatcher was proud of defeating an oppressive regime — soon after the war the dictatorship ended.

The Gulf War, 1990–1991

Phew. The <u>last</u> and <u>most recent</u> of the wars you need to cover — be sure you learn <u>all</u> the facts.

Iraq was short of money, and Kuwait had plenty

1) During the <u>1980s</u>, the Middle Eastern country of Iraq had fought a <u>long war</u> against its neighbour Iran. When the war ended in <u>1988</u>, Iraq needed cash to <u>rebuild</u>.

2) The Iraqi leader, the dictator <u>Saddam Hussein</u>, accused the small <u>oil-rich country</u> of <u>Kuwait</u> of ripping Iraq off in oil sales. He claimed Kuwait <u>historically belonged</u> to Iraq.

Iraq invaded Kuwait on August 3 1990

1) Efforts by <u>neighbouring countries</u> to solve the quarrel with talks came to nothing. An Iraqi army of 150 000 was sent to the Kuwaiti border. The Kuwaiti army had only 20 000 men.

2) On <u>August 3 1990</u>, the Iraqis had captured Kuwait City, and went on to take the whole country.

3) The United Nations ordered <u>economic sanctions</u> against Iraq — nobody would trade with them.

4) But <u>Kuwait</u> sells a lot of <u>oil</u> to the West. Now Western countries could <u>no longer buy oil</u> from Kuwait.

5) **OPERATION DESERT SHIELD:** Western countries, including the <u>USA</u>, <u>Britain</u>, and <u>France</u> joined up with many <u>Arab countries</u> including <u>Saudi Arabia</u> and <u>Egypt</u> to fight Iraq. 600 000 soldiers including 400 000 from the US gathered in <u>Saudi Arabia</u>.

6) Iraq threatened to use <u>chemical weapons</u>, to <u>attack civilians</u> in cities, and to <u>use prisoners</u> taken in Kuwait as '<u>human shields</u>' to defend their military bases.

7) On <u>29 November</u>, the <u>UN Security Council</u> issued an ultimatum to Iraq. If they didn't get out of Kuwait by <u>15 January</u> a United Nations force would <u>make</u> them leave using "all necessary means".

The war started with air attacks, and ended with land battles

1) Iraq made no move to get out of Kuwait. At a meeting between the <u>Iraqi</u> and <u>US</u> Foreign Secretaries the <u>US</u> made it plain that they <u>weren't afraid</u> to go to <u>war</u>.

2) **DESERT STORM:** On <u>17 January 1991</u>, the <u>Coalition</u> launched <u>massive air attacks</u> on Iraq, destroying their air force quickly. Iraq responded by launching Scud missiles on <u>civilian targets</u> in <u>Israel</u> and <u>Saudi Arabia</u>.

3) **DESERT SABRE:** A <u>land attack</u> began on <u>24 February</u>. Coalition forces attacked the Iraqi army in Kuwait and Southern Iraq. Another group moved up the coast and <u>liberated Kuwait</u>.

4) Many thousands of Iraqis <u>surrendered</u> or <u>deserted</u>. The rest of the army <u>set light</u> to Kuwaiti <u>oil wells</u> as they withdrew. There were lakes of oil and massive clouds of smoke creating terrible pollution.

5) A <u>ceasefire</u> was declared on <u>28 February</u>.

OVERALL RESULTS

1) About <u>240 Coalition troops</u> were <u>killed</u>. There are <u>no official figures</u> from <u>Iraq</u>, but there could have been between 10 000 and 100 000 dead.

2) <u>Kurds</u> in the North of Iraq and <u>Shiite Muslims</u> in the South revolted against Saddam Hussein straight after the war, but got <u>no help</u> from abroad.

3) Many British and American Gulf veterans have had <u>health problems</u> — called <u>Gulf War Syndrome</u>. It may have been caused by chemical or biological weapons or by depleted uranium ammunition.

4) The West could <u>buy Kuwait's oil</u> again. Some people said it was the <u>only</u> real reason for the war.

5) Kuwait's Royal Family promised democracy after the war, but the country still <u>isn't a democracy</u> by European or American standards.

6) The <u>US took the lead</u> in the Coalition. Britain was seen to <u>follow the US policy</u>, and <u>didn't act alone</u>.

7) Iraq was invaded <u>again</u> by US and British forces on <u>March 20th, 2003</u>. This was the start of the <u>Iraq War</u>. Saddam Hussein was <u>removed</u> as president and put on trial for <u>human rights abuses</u>. There's still a lot of <u>unrest</u> in Iraq, and UK and US troops stayed on to <u>keep the peace</u>.

Three different situations — three roles for Britain to play...

Scribble a <u>quick list</u> of the <u>main facts</u> about each of the 3 wars or crises in this section. Be ready for questions about <u>how</u> Britain's role <u>changed</u> between Suez, the Falklands and the Gulf...

Revision Summary

Suez, the Falklands and the Gulf show three different sides to Britain — Britain as a fading world power in Suez; Britain acting decisively and alone in the Falklands; and Britain as part of an international Coalition, following the USA's lead, in the Gulf. There's a lot of stuff to learn here — you don't have to be an expert on each conflict, but you need to know the causes and the main results. Have a go at these questions, go back over the section and try them again. You should be able to answer every one of them if you want to do well in the Exam.

1) Why was the Suez canal important to Britain?

2) What happened in Egypt in 1952?

3) Why did the USA refuse to help Egypt pay for the Aswan dam?

   a) Eygpt was too corrupt. b) It would ruin the Nile river. c) Egypt was buying Russian weapons

4) What did Nasser do in 1956 to find the money to pay for the dam?

5) Give one reason why the British Cabinet, the French Government and MI6 wanted strong action to be taken against Nasser immediately?

6) What was the secret pact between Britain, France and Israel?

7) What was the reaction of the USA and USSR to the attack on Egypt?

8) Give two overall results of the Suez Crisis.

9) How did the crisis make Britain appear to the rest of the world?

10) When did Argentina invade the Falkland Islands?

11) How many ships and men made up the British Task Force?

12) What was the Total Exclusion Zone?

13) Why was the sinking of the *General Belgrano* so controversial?

14) Give two overall results of the Falklands War.

15) How did the crisis make Britain appear to the rest of the world?

16) Why did Iraq need cash after 1988?

17) What was Operation Desert Shield?

18) What was Operation Desert Storm?

19) What was Operation Desert Sabre?

20) Give two overall results of the Gulf War.

21) What was Britain's role in the Coalition?

22) What are the main similarities and differences between Britain's roles in the Suez Crisis, the Falklands War and the Gulf War?

Mmmm...I could get well into this Operation Desert Sabre.

Index

Index